AMERICAN
BEST SELLERS

A M E R I C A N
Best Sellers

A READER'S GUIDE
TO POPULAR FICTION

Karen Hinckley and Barbara Hinckley

INDIANA

UNIVERSITY

PRESS

Bloomington & Indianapolis

MANUFACTURED IN THE UNITED STATES OF AMERICA

Library of Congress Cataloging-in-Publication Data

Hinckley, Karen
American best sellers.

Bibliography: p.
Includes index.
1. American fiction—20th century—Stories, plots,
etc.   2. American fiction—20th century—Bibliography.
3. Best sellers—United States—Stories, plots, etc.
4. Best sellers—United States—Bibliography.
5. Popular literature—United States—Stories, plots,
etc.   6. Popular literature—United States—Bibliography.   7. Books and reading—United States—History—
20th century.   I. Hinckley, Barbara.
II. Title.
PS374.B45H56   1989   813'.54'09   88–45754

ISBN 0–253–32728–8

1 2 3 4 5 93 92 91 90 89

)-14-91

C O N T E N T S

Authors' Note

The idea for this book occurred to both authors suddenly and simultaneously. It swiftly grew into a two-year project, eclipsing all other work and all other reading. The manuscript endured through various types of mutilation by dogs and cats in Wisconsin, and went on to survive being mailed into and out of New York City. Now that the idea has become a book, the authors wish to thank Elizabeth Reinartz for her fine teaching years ago, the staff of the Sequoya Branch of the Madison Public Library, and the availability of the Strand Bookstore. Thanks also to everyone at Indiana who gave their usual superlative job of production.

AMERICAN
BEST SELLERS

Introduction

EVERYONE READS best sellers, but no one knows very much about them. No comprehensive guide lists the books all together, gives details about the authors, or shows the trends across time. Whereas moviegoers have many such guides available, book readers do not. They might have missed, for example, a book by their favorite mystery writer or one of last week's arrivals from Stephen King. They might like to see which books have won Pulitzer Prizes or which repeat the same plot five times in a row. People buy them, scorn them, wait for the next one, and give advice on how to write them, without really knowing what the best sellers are like.

This book offers a comprehensive look at best-selling hardcover fiction of the past 20 years. It allows people to read more about the authors and the books, and to identify major topics and trends. It is based on the *World Almanac*'s annual listing of books highest in U.S. sales—approximately 20 to 30 books a year. It is these top sellers we will be concerned with here: altogether, 468 books and 216 authors in the 20-year period. Since the list is based on U.S. sales and publication efforts, we call them American best sellers, whatever the nationalities of the authors. Books by Agatha Christie are American best sellers, and so is the translation of Umberto Eco's *The Name of the Rose*.

It is curious that no such basic account has been readily available before this.[1] Reviewers of popular fiction typically select the books they want to talk about, ignoring others or remaining unaware of them. The bookstores themselves are of little help. A book missed once is lost to view and soon joins the limbo of last year's best sellers. Neutral accounts, too, are hard to come by. Critics treat best sellers as automatically suspect, while publishers are financially motivated to praise them. No one covers the middle ground. In some cases, in fact, it is difficult to discover what a book is about. Ignored by reviewers, the book can be known only by its cover and promotion campaign.

The cover of *Such Good Friends* announces that "Julie embarks on a sexual odyssey of vengeance unparalleled in modern marriage, recent fiction, and wildest fantasy!" In the actual novel, however, there is no sexual odyssey at all, let alone an unparalleled one. Julie's adventures are limited to sleeping with her husband's friend in one unsuccessful evening. What she really does is maintain a vigil outside her unfaithful husband's hospital room and look back at her life and marriage. People waiting for that odyssey will be disappointed, to say the least, while those who might like to know how the character copes with the double disaster that has struck will never get past the cover.

But more basically, people miss what the books are like because of the stereotyping of best sellers. Critic Edmund Wilson praises best-selling author Edwin O'Connor and admits, " . . . a literary intellectual objects to nothing so much as a best-selling book that also possesses real merit."[2] Best sellers, *as a category*, are set apart from books that possess merit. The same kind of categorization is found in a *Writer's Digest* piece entitled "How to Write Blockbuster Novels." Best sellers, according to the author, should have plots that can be summarized in one sentence, action that maintains a state of perpetual high drama, and characters who are unambivalent. We hate them or we adore them. Forget being a stylist, the author urges, and forget details of background and atmosphere. Two of the models suggested, not surprisingly, are Harold Robbins and Jacqueline Susann.[3] Yet many of the best sellers do rely on details of background and atmosphere: Thomas Tryon's *The Other* and *Harvest Home*, for example, or any of the novels by John Fowles. Many of the books show very complex characters. We do not hate or adore the protagonists in *The Embezzler* or *The Rector of Justin.* The two critics are poles apart as reviewers of fiction, but the stereotyping is the same.

This book will attempt to correct the information gap that exists for American best-selling novels. A review of the top 468 best sellers from 1965 through 1985, it should provide a clearer sense of what the books are like—in their range and diversity and their elements in common. It should also give the kind of basic information that people can use to see at a glance what the best sellers have been—and draw up their own lists and conclusions.

What are the best sellers and what are they like? Who writes them, and what do they deal with? Can we generalize about their themes and characters, or are the differences more striking than the similarities? These questions are of interest not only to potential readers but to students of popular culture. With the changes in society from the 1960s to the 1980s, how have the best sellers changed? Who, for example, are the heroes and heroines, what battles do they fight, and what dreams do they pursue? This book will answer these questions by identifying major topics and trends. Some beginning answers, however, can be offered by way of introduction to show the diversity of the books and set the context for the following chapters.

What Is a Best Seller?

The one thing these books have in common is a very high sales figure over a short period of time, usually not exceeding one year. A book is commonly called a best seller if its hardcover sales reach 100,000 copies and paperback sales 1,000,000. The top sellers do considerably better. However, these range from serious literature to highly intelligent escape reading, on through the ranks of formula fiction to drivel. One magazine nominated three best sellers as the worst book of the year for 1968: Drury's *Preserve and Protect*, Drew Pearson's *The Senator,* and Gore Vidal's *Myra Breckinridge*. An even more spirited competition for worst book might be waged by some of the best sellers of the 1980s, where, for example, characters we do not care about work their way through enough boardrooms and bedrooms until the pages contracted for have been completed. At the other extreme, six Pulitzer Prize winners are also best sellers: Saul Bellow's *Humboldt's Gift*; *The Stories of John Cheever*; Bernard Malamud's *The Fixer*; *The Confessions of Nat Turner* by William Styron; Norman Mailer's *The Executioner's Song*; and John Updike's *Rabbit Is Rich*.

Many of the formulas for best sellers can be questioned by looking through the books on the list. Sex, for example, is often seen as a requirement for a best-selling novel, with the book highest in individual sales, Jacqueline Susann's *Valley of the Dolls*, used to support this assertion. But to make a convincing argument against this point, look at the three authors ranked highest in the number of best sellers written. Victoria Holt's heroines find suspense and romance, Stephen King's characters face terror and the supernatural, and Robert Ludlum's heroes are caught in gigantic international conspiracies, all with sex used very infrequently in the stories. Holt has 10 books and King and Ludlum 9 each in the 20-year period.

The characters are as diverse as the themes and categories. They range from Russian spies to small-town rabbis, from Gothic heroines to Green Berets. Sometimes the same stock character, with only the name and circumstances changed, will appear in several stories. But we also find such original detectives as Miss Marple, the Russian Arkady Renko, and Sergeant Valnikov with his drinking problem and 19-year-long nightmare. Bellow created the unique Moses Herzog, who writes unmailed letters to people

(Nietzsche, Eisenhower, his deceased relatives, former mistresses) as he fights through a personal crisis, restores his house in the country, and thinks of murdering his wife's lover.

There is a striking diversity among the authors, too. Best sellers are written by former vice-presidents, Nobel Prize winners, missionaries, and scientists; elderly ladies, farm girls, and feminists; lawyers, teachers, and cops. It is interesting that 63, or 30% of the authors are women—a higher proportion than is found in most other high-paying professions. People know of the repeating authors, who publish a best seller every year or two. But more than half of the authors appear with their first best seller, and for a few it is the only book they have written.

Some are full-time and some are part-time writers. Asimov writes 4,000 words a day, while Graham Greene tries for 400, although he says they will need rewriting. Irving Stone works daily on his books from 9:00 to 6:00 with only a short break for lunch. Louis Auchincloss, however, writes his best sellers while pursuing a full-time career as a Wall Street lawyer, and Father Andrew Greeley divides his time between writing, teaching sociology, and the church. Colleen McCullough wrote *The Thorn Birds* from evening to dawn after a day's work at the Yale neurological laboratory. It was therapy, she said, in the wake of an unhappy love affair. Joseph Wambaugh stayed on the force of the Los Angeles Police Department after becoming a best-selling novelist. He claims he resigned finally after a suspect he was arresting asked for an audition for "Police Story".[4]

Some authors engage in extensive research. Alexander Solzhenitsyn's *August 1914*, for example, is the product of a major study of military history and strategy. It has been praised for the detail of its battle plans and knowledge of military science. Even so, the author points out in the Foreword that the book is only the beginning of a larger study which will take 20 more years to complete. Erica Jong's *Fanny*, which gives a contemporary feminist view of the adventures of an 18th-century character, grew out of her graduate work in literature. Jong turns the original Woman of Pleasure of John Cleland's *Fanny Hill* into a courageous heroine while capturing the language and spirit of an 18th-century novel. Ruth Beebe Hill's *Hanta Yo* is based on a lifelong study of American Indians, during which time she lived with the tribes and learned their dialects. Michener also supplies fascinating detail in each of his books. Just read the list of credits in any one of them.

At the other extreme, Leon Uris admits that a "crash course in history" is all that it takes to write his historical novels. He sees them as transported westerns with no real research needed. Martin Cruz Smith drew compliments for his authentic portrayal of Russian daily life in *Gorky Park*. Smith, however, who speaks no Russian, visited the country for only five days in 1973. He did read widely about Soviet law enforcement and talked to Russian emigres in New York.

In many cases the author's imagination serves as a successful substitute for research. Elmore Leonard, best-selling author of *Glitz*, who wanted inside information on the work of a hotel thief, asked the assistance of a chief of security in a large metropolitan hotel. When the security man declined to help—no doubt envisioning the instructions on how to burglarize a hotel suddenly made available to millions of readers—Leonard decided to "make it up." He has also made up the dialogue of underworld characters, arguments between ball players, and the procedure for handling cash in a large department store. However he does it, people seem to agree that most of the details are right.[5]

The authors' attitudes toward their work are different as well. There is a great distance indeed from a John Updike or Eudora Welty, who treat the art of the novel seriously and self-consciously, to some of their neighbors on the best-selling lists. In contrast to the serious literary novelists, consider Lawrence Sanders's puzzled reaction to a highly favorable *New York Times* review. Said Sanders, "I don't take myself seriously, so why should anyone else? I'm writing entertainment—I hope intelligent entertainment, but that's all." And when Greeley was attacked for the sensationalism in his books, he said simply, "I am telling the kind of story I want to tell the way I want to tell it, to people who like such stories, and that seems to me quite enough."[6]

In other cases, authors combine the goal of entertainment with a message they feel strongly about. Ludlum clearly entertains, with nine best sellers in 12 years through 1984. Yet his books convey a sense of moral outrage at what international power elites—consisting of governments, industrialists, and financiers—are capable of doing. In *The Rhinemann Exchange* Germans and Americans arrange a trade to keep World War II going. In *The Matarese Circle* an international group plans simultaneous takeovers of the major world governments, and in *The Holcroft Covenant* another international group plots to establish a Fourth Reich. As Ludlum admits in an end note reprinted in several of the novels, "I write primarily as an entertainer. But . . . you write from a point of view of something that disturbs or outrages you. And that's what I do. I admit to being outraged—mostly by the abuse of power by the fanatics."

Even more clearly, Allen Drury has a message to tell in his books on American politics. Drury is strongly opposed to a foreign policy he sees as appeasing Communism and sharply critical of the press. The villains in his stories are primarily journalists and liberal presidential candidates. As he explains to the reader in *Preserve and Protect*, he is "continuing the argument between those who favor the responsible use of strength to oppose the Communist drive for world dominion, and those who believe that in a reluctance to be firm, in permissiveness, and in the steady erosion of the law lies the surest path to a secure and stable world society." For Drury, entertainment does not require a careful balance of points of view.

On the other hand, there are writers whose message is only the story itself and whose primary goal is to tell it. Three years before his death, John O'Hara observed in *And Other Stories* that the worst thing about growing old was the diminished strength for his work. He added, "Much as I like owning a Rolls Royce . . . I could do without it. What I could not do without is a typewriter, a supply of yellow second sheets, and the time to put them to good use." Michener, too, regrets that he may not have time to do a book on the Caribbean or all the other land masses and eons of geologic deposits whose stories should be told. And when Graham Greene was asked what he would like to accomplish as a writer, he answered simply, "Just write a good book."[7]

If it seems startling to invoke Updike and Sanders, or Drury and Greene, in the same paragraph, the point should be clear. They all have written best sellers. So Vidal reviews "The Ten Top Best Sellers" of 1973, beginning with the eye-catching line "Shit has its own integrity." Assigned the review one year later, he would be criticizing himself. Number one in 1973 was *Jonathan Livingston Seagull*. (Vidal calls it "a greeting card bound like a book.") Number one the following year was *Burr*.[8]

At the same time, some books are more likely to appear on the best-seller lists than others. There are dominant themes and character types; some categories are more popular than others. While the books are diverse, they can be grouped by genre, topic, and the appeal they make to readers.

When the books are divided according to genre and topic, the most popular category is clear. This group consists of the historical novels, books with settings before World War I. A second large category comprises the dynasty novels: sagas of families over several generations. The plots are typically simple, telling of a rise from rags to riches, or the futility of riches, or a power struggle within a family. The characters are often only briefly sketched, since three or more generations of marriages and deaths, triumphs and failures, secret deals and murderous secrets must be recounted before the novel's conclusion. Nevertheless, they offer the reader a kind of instant history, too. The families are shown against the sweep of events from the coming of the industrial age, through depression and war, to the modern era.

In addition, there are more than 20 books apiece in such familiar categories as spy novels, mysteries, and tales of horror and the supernatural, but few science-fiction stories and westerns. The rarity of science-fiction books is interesting, given the popularity of science-fiction films. In fact, two of the best-selling books—*E.T.* and *Return of the Jedi*—were written in book form only after they succeeded at theaters. Arranging the best sellers by topic, we find a large number of books about American politics and international intrigue, as well as the stories set during or immediately after World War II. Presidents are defeated, blinded, kidnapped, and assassinated. Senators sell out. Journalists fight coverups or contribute to them. There is corruption in Washington, fighting in the Middle East, conspiracy by international cartels, terrorism, and the threat of nuclear war. Readers are not only getting some instant history; they are getting a crash course in current events, too. Whether the courses are accurate is an entirely different matter.

Then there are books on sex and Hollywood glamour, as everyone might expect. But, contrary to expectations, we find in chapter 2 that these categories are no more popular than many others, and less popular than some.

At the other extreme, very few satires, comedies, or collections of short stories appear on the lists, and few books about American wars other than World War II. Only two children's books are best sellers—*The Butter Battle Book* and *Nutcracker*—again in marked contrast to the movie and video industry. (The book *E.T.* has language and details of characterization that might require a PG-13 movie rating.) Still, almost half of the best sellers do not fit clear genre categories, so a good deal of diversity remains.

Cutting across the categories, however, we find other similarities. If books are grouped according to their appeal to readers, a large majority of the best sellers offer one or more of the following rewards. They offer factual information, the kind of escape reading that comes from predictability, or the satisfaction of experiencing in fictional form some common dreams and nightmares of American life.

Fiction as Fact: Learning Can Be Fun

Many of the novels claim to be useful as well as entertaining. Whether they feature inside accounts or years of research, they offer factual information in the easily palatable form of the fictional story. Novels by insiders take us within an industry or occupation or group to show "how it really is." Officer Wambaugh tells us how policemen think; Potok gives details of a rabbi's daily life; presidential aides Safire and Salinger show what goes on in the White House. One way, it is clear, to write a best-selling novel is to have another career to tell people about.

Authors lacking an interesting background are free to research one, or to make up the details, as long as the effect of authenticity is achieved. Thus, we find pages of maps, bibliographies, and long lists of credits to convince readers that they are getting new and substantial information along with their story. Arthur Hailey shows the inside workings of numerous industries, including an airport, a power company, a bank, and a hospital. The only information most people have about power companies is how much they charge a month—or their policy on disconnect notices. *Overload*, then, can offer a behind-the-scenes look at the complex workings of a power company and the continuing problems it faces. Michael Crichton scatters charts, computer messages, and technical appendixes throughout his novels. While the material has little to do with the story or its supposed scientific subject matter, it can help foster the impression that serious information is being provided.

We can now see why historical novels and books about current events are so popular. Along with accounts of industries and occupations, special groups and scientific experiments, they offer more than a story. Readers can justify the time spent on entertainment by being informed. "We Americans," one critic points out, "are reluctant to take our fiction straight without a chaser of education."[9]

The popularity of these books is seen in the promotions suggesting that the fiction may actually be fact. The novels are cast as predictions of next year's headlines or thinly disguised accounts of real persons and events. The cover promotion for *The Day of the Jackal* asks, "Can This Be Fiction?" with the implication that it is not. *The Last Days of America* is called "as real as today's headlines," and *The Spike* is said to be "so convincing that it's hard to tell where fact leaves off and fiction begins." The books themselves may offer routine information that is available to the most occasional newspaper reader, or plots that are bizarre and incredible. Maybe there are 171 Russian KGB agents in the White House alone, as *The Spike* tells us. Or maybe there are not. Fiction writers are free to imagine whatever they want.

The novels, in fact, vary tremendously in the amount of information and misinformation they convey. Member of Parliament Jeffrey Archer wrote *First among Equals*, a story of three men who compete to be the British prime minister. Most of the book, however, relies on basic information that one need not be a British politician to know. The same can be said for the vice-presidency in Agnew's *The Canfield Decision*. On the other hand, in *Full Disclosure*, William Safire writes about routines and strategies of the Nixon White House that could be known only by insiders. In *The Triumph*, Galbraith offers a rare look inside the State Department bureaucracy. His 1968 fictional account of the Martinez regime sounds like the Philippines of the Marcoses nearly 20 years later. But even in the 1960s, American political conventions were far from the free-for-alls that Knebel and Drury would have their readers believe. In Knebel's *Dark Horse*, deadlocked convention members finally turn to Eddie Quinn, a New Jersey turnpike commissioner, to be their presidential nominee. The last dark horse actually nominated at a convention was Wendell Willkie in 1940, hardly a turnpike commissioner, and before that one would have to go back to 1924, when the rules of the convention were very different. Nor are vice-presidents and cabinet members just waiting for the chance to snatch power from a disabled or missing president. Their real problem would be to get in to *see* the presidents, never mind to overthrow them.

In each of these cases readers are offered information along with the story, but, as the book covers say, it is hard to know where fact stops and the fiction begins.

Formula Fiction: No More Surprises

Some best sellers offer predictability rather than information. Readers have had enough surprises and challenges for one day, and enough information, too. They want to relax with a good book and not be disappointed. They know the author already, the hero, and perhaps even the outline of the plot. Many of the best-selling detective and spy stories offer this kind of escape reading. People know Lew Archer or Hercule Poirot and do not need to think about a new character. In a John MacDonald mystery, they know Travis McGee, his friends, and his very personal code of honor. Travis sails his boat in the Florida Keys, uncovers a series of murders, and gives his own comments about what is wrong with the world. Readers of a William Buckley spy novel already know CIA agent Blackford Oakes. They know what to expect from the author's wit and can look forward to another imaginary conversation between presidents, foreign-policy advisers, and other famous people. The predictability is deliberate in these cases and a large part of the books' appeal.

The number of these books among the top best sellers attests to their popularity. Buckley and Christie have five each, and MacDonald has five in the Travis McGee series alone. Robert Ludlum accounts for nine of the spy stories, each pitting a fairly ordinary American against a gigantic international conspiracy. Even the titles are predictable and, like all good formulas, easily interchangeable (*The Holcroft Covenant; The Aquitaine Progression; The Parsifal Mosaic*, and on through the rest of the three-word titles). Lawrence Sanders has written six of the best-selling mysteries, and still has some of the Ten Commandments and the seven deadly sins to go.

It is not only the mysteries and spy stories, however, that offer this kind of predictability. Arthur Hailey's books supply formula as well as fact. In each of his six best sellers he assembles a collection of characters and shows us their backgrounds, ambitions, and fears. The heroes and villains are instantly recognizable. Community groups—working for civil rights, the environment, or the prevention of cruelty to animals—agitate briefly and are unsuccessful. To this basic brew Hailey adds all the details of the various work establishments and enough crisis to keep the action at highest pitch. The industries are changed, from hotel to airport to hospital, while the rest of the book remains the same. Another example of formula fiction is provided by Robin Cook. Cook's novels are a cross between a Gothic horror story and *General Hospital*. In three best sellers (*Coma, Brain*, and *Godplayer*), something is very wrong at a large metropolitan hospital. A female physician must discover what it is and risk her career and romance in the process. The novels end with the doctor-heroine herself a patient, vulnerable and in need of rescue. The same plot, in fact, appears three times with only the names of the characters changed.

Fantasy Fiction: Imagine That . . .

Another kind of escape allows readers to face their dreams and nightmares in fictional form. Many of the books portray fantasy lives of the rich and famous. Details of character and plot are kept to a minimum so that reality cannot break through to spoil the fantasy. The men are rich, powerful, and sexually successful (Robbins), while the women are young, beautiful film stars (Susann) or the young, beautiful wives of film stars (Collins). Other books, too, allow readers to escape from paying their bills to a world where wealth can be taken for granted. Louis Auchincloss, with five best sellers, describes a world of money and position in New York society. Paul Erdman's heroes travel the globe making financial deals that change the course of nations. In other books fame and political power are the subjects of fantasy. According to the top sellers, Washington, D.C., and Hollywood are the glamour capitals of the world. So family money lets characters run for the presidency (*All in the Family*; *The Prodigal Daughter*; *Captains and the Kings*), while stories about policemen and authors, murder and incest are given Hollywood settings. Altogether, more than 50 of the top best sellers deal primarily with money, fame in film or politics, or other kinds of glamour.

Even more of the books project the rags-to-riches fantasy of the American Dream (see chapter 5). People pursue life, liberty, and property in a land where all things are possible. The dream appears in different forms, whether it is the classic rags-to-riches story or merely the background of a minor character. It is pursued by individuals and across several generations of a family. In *Kane and Abel*, Abel Rosnovski, a Polish orphan born to poverty, immigrates to the United States, goes to night school while he works as a waiter, and rises to become a hotel tycoon. He will come to rival William Kane, who was born to wealth and privilege, went to Harvard while Abel was going to night school, and made his first million before he graduated from college. Most of the family sagas show the dream at work across several generations. In the novels of Howard Fast, for example, the hardworking immigrants give birth to the upwardly mobile second generation, who in turn produce the tycoons and dynasties of the present day. Throughout the sagas the immigrants come from different lands and face different circumstances, but the Horatio Alger story is the same.

The best-selling nightmares are more diverse; still, some themes appear with unusual frequency. Four in particular are interesting to watch for. The American Dream can go wrong or turn into a nightmare. Characters suddenly find that "something happened": they have been led into a dead end or trap of their own making. In other books, scientists are out of control, scattering deadly germs or conducting brain transplants in large hospitals. In still others, giant conspiracies exist, linking governments, banks, and other power centers, against which the individual is helpless. The glories of technology and politics, like the American Dream itself, have their darker side. Supernatural horrors also exist, although they appear with less frequency. They are found lurking in quiet Maine villages, waiting for young couples in Manhattan apartments, or possessing little girls in bedrooms in Georgetown. In each of these cases readers can face their own fears in the guise of a fictional story.

Best sellers are not unique in offering escape, information, and vicarious experience. All fiction can provide these, along with other effects. The best sellers, however, are very *specific* in the kind of information and escape they offer and in the recurring dreams and nightmares that appear. While the books cannot be stereotyped, they can be analyzed for their specific themes and treatments. These will be seen more clearly in the following chapters.

One caution is important at the outset. As we look at the best sellers throughout this book, we cannot say these are what the public wants: American readers like such and such a thing or they are turning away from something else. We can only say what the best sellers are. Publishers can decide to promote a book into a top seller, with the publicity tours arranged before the manuscript is done. This occurred with Jacqueline Susann's *Valley of the Dolls*, to name only one of many examples. Book clubs make or break best sellers when they decide, long before the book is in print, what their members will be offered to read. A group of New York Times critics "discovered" Ross Macdonald after he had been writing mysteries for many years. So *The Goodbye Look* was given the lead review under the banner "The Finest Detective Novel Ever Written," catapulting Macdonald from a typical mystery writer with his loyal coterie of fans into a best-selling author. In none of these cases are the readers deciding what the best-selling books will be. Stranded at the airport or on their way home from work, they are picking the best book for them that is available. They might criticize the best sellers, too, and wish they had better books to choose from.

A dramatic example of how best sellers are created is provided by the books of Louis L'Amour. For forty years L'Amour wrote paperback westerns, with nearly 100 titles in print by the 1980s. Then, when Ronald Reagan was president, L'Amour was awarded the Presidential Medal of Freedom for his writing. Suddenly, for the first time in six decades, a hardcover western was published—*The Lonesome Gods*.[10] This became L'Amour's first top selling novel, because that is what it was expected and promoted to be.

Still, some books that are vigorously promoted do not sell well; the same authors do better with some books than others. The reading public is not merely a passive recipient here—its "votes," in the form of purchases, do make a difference. Just as in the electoral process people select within a limited set of candidates the ones they would most like in office, book buyers have a real, though limited, influence. And just as politicians must constantly watch what the voters are looking for, publishers must watch the readers.

We thus find two effects which will be seen throughout the following chapters. There is a *diversity* of books overall, with different types published for various target audiences (those who like mysteries or spy stories or historical novels). While the types are similar in themselves—in their characters, their plots, and even in their authors—each type is distinct from the others. There is also *continuity*. The book industry conducts little market research on the likes and dislikes of its consumers: hence the best guides to the future are the sales figures of the past. But this means that the same authors and the same kind of books will continue across the years. One successful book leads to others. So the best sellers one finds on the bookstore displays are predictions, rather than results, of a popularity contest. They show what the industry *thinks* the public wants based on the choices that were made before. Those choices, too, were limited by estimates of what the readers wanted then.

Guide to the Book

This book is designed to be comprehensive and informative. We have thus remained primarily neutral, letting the books as far as possible speak for themselves. We have also tried to balance the need to cover this very large subject with enough supporting detail and example. We concentrate on major themes and topics only, as seen by the frequency of books in the various categories, and use representative examples along with briefer references to other books. This means that many interesting questions and minor themes cannot be covered and that some books which have inspired whole bibliographies of commentary will be mentioned only briefly. People seeking more information can turn to the reading list at the end of this volume.

Readers will be able to use this book to gain information without reading from cover to cover or in any particular order. Thus the explanation of terms and sources needed for each chapter is found within the chapter itself. The book is organized to present the basic information first, in chapters 1 through 3, followed by short essays on characters, themes, and current trends in chapters 4 through 6.

Chapter 1 supplies the complete listing of the top sellers from 1965 to 1985. The list is arranged alphabetically by author with a short description of each book, its category, and publishing information. Each entry also includes brief biographical information on the authors, including little-known facts and other fiction they have written. In many cases the authors' lives are as interesting as their books: there are doctors of medicine, deep-sea divers, a teacher in the Australian Outback, and a mother of nine children. Seeing the books all together is quite revealing too. For some authors publishing a best seller is an annual routine. Some stay with the same story line with only the names of the characters changed, while others experiment with different kinds of writing. Further information about the authors is provided in chapter 2.

Chapter 3 shows the books by topic and genre and defines the categories. It looks at the most frequently appearing categories and asks how these have changed over time. It also lists the books in the most popular categories, telling something about the past history of the genre and its famous practitioners. Here, for example, those who like mysteries can see all these books at a glance, along with the names of the most popular detectives. Those who like historical novels can find more than 70 books to choose from and see the century and locale of their setting.

The following chapters draw this information together to highlight major patterns and trends. In the chapter on characters, for example, we ask who the heroes are. We look at the small select group of heroines, and compare the villain to the faceless enemy. The chapter on themes identifies, among other topics, frequently occurring nightmares, and traces three decades of the American Dream. The final chapter includes the best sellers published since 1985 and looks at trends across time. This chapter will reveal several surprises; some kinds of books have faded from view, while others are reemerging. Nevertheless, it is as interesting to see the things that do not change as those that do. Many of the older authors remain on the bookstore shelves in 1987, while the newest books on the list looks strangely like those we have read before.

In short, this book provides a guide for readers, along with some general signposts, so that they can see what the best sellers are like. As a book about books, it can be used as a reference, or a shopping list, or even be read on its own.

N O T E S

1. The book by Alice Hackett *Eighty Years of Best Sellers* (New York: R. R. Bowker, 1977) ends with 1975 and is out of print. Hackett merely lists books by year and supplies little other information. John Sutherland, *Bestsellers: Popular Fiction of the 1970s* (London: Routledge & Kegan Paul, 1981), selects books to talk about within the decade of the 1970s, but does not work from any comprehensive list. Other sources report the top best sellers annually (*World Almanac*) or weekly (*Publishers Weekly*, the *New York Times*) but do not provide any overall listing.

2. *The Best and Last of Edwin O'Connor* (Boston: Little, Brown, 1969), p. 346.

3. Evan Marshall, "How to Write Blockbuster Novels," *Writer's Digest*, October 1986, pp. 30–33.

4. For McCullough, see *World Authors, 1975–1980*, p. 464; for Wambaugh, see *Time* magazine, June 8, 1981, p. 79.

5. For Uris, see Sutherland, p. 207; for Smith and Leonard, see Peter Prescott, *Never in Doubt* (New York: Arbor House, 1986), pp. 112, 113; 92, 93.

6. Interview with Lawrence Sanders, *Publishers Weekly*, August 2, 1976, quoted in Sutherland, p. 229; for Greeley, see *Confessions of a Parish Priest* (New York: Pocket Books, 1987), p. 493.

7. For the interviews with Michener and Greene, see Al Silverman, ed., *The Book of the Month* (Boston: Little, Brown, 1986), pp. 274, 222.

8. Gore Vidal, "The Top Best Sellers of 1973," reprinted in *Matters of Fact and of Fiction* (New York: Vintage, 1977), pp. 3–26. The books were ranked first according to the *World Almanac*'s ranking for 1973 and 1974.

9. Prescott, p. 111.

10. *Publishers Weekly*, March 16, 1984, p. 29.

The Main Listing of Books

HERE ARE THE TOP fictional best sellers from 1965 to 1985, arranged alphabetically by author. (The books published later than 1985 are listed in chapter 6, "The Trends Today.") Each entry supplies facts about the author and a short description of the book, including its category by genre or subject matter. The copyright page of the hardcover book is the main source for publication information and the spelling of the author's name. The first U.S. edition is used. Where the spelling is inconsistent across several books, we have followed the *Contemporary Authors* series listing. Where two publishers are listed on the copyright page, we have taken the more inclusive of the two: i.e., the parent firm and not the division. The author entries have been compiled from many different sources, as reported in the bibliography at the end of the book. A question mark following a birth date means that the question mark was used in the original and is the best information available. The categories used to describe the books are explained further in the following chapter, but in most cases they should speak for themselves.

ADAMS, DOUGLAS

Born in England, 1952; educated at St. Johns College, Cambridge. He has written for television and worked as a radio producer, script editor, and bodyguard. Adams is the author of the *Hitchhiker*'s series, which includes *The Hitchhiker's Guide to the Galaxy*; *The Restaurant at the End of the Universe*; *Life, the Universe, and Everything*; and *So Long, and Thanks for All the Fish*. He also wrote *Dirk Gently's Holistic Detective Agency*.

So Long, and Thanks for All the Fish   CROWN, 1984
Science Fiction. The latest book in Adams's offbeat series finds Arthur Dent returning to Earth, years after its apparent destruction. He falls in love with a girl who has a secret, and they journey to California to find out why the dolphins said, "So long, and thanks for all the fish."

ADAMS, RICHARD
Born in England, 1920. He was educated at Oxford, and served in the British army from 1940 to 46. Adams is a Fellow of the Royal Society of Literature and a member of the Royal Society for the Prevention of Cruelty to Animals. He won the Guardian Award for children's literature in 1972, and is also the author of *The Plague Dogs* and *Maia*.

Watership Down   MACMILLAN, 1974
Adventure. A suspenseful tale of rabbits who must leave their home to find and build a new warren. Along the way they plan strategies, recount legends, and contend with other animals and evil rabbits. The book can be enjoyed by people of all ages and levels of sophistication. Includes a Lapine Glossary and maps.

Shardik   SIMON & SCHUSTER, 1974
Historical Novel–Adventure. Routed by fire, a great bear wanders into contact with human beings in the primitive Beklan Empire. Named Shardik, or the Power of God, he is worshipped by some, imprisoned and tortured by others and inspires the solitary hunter Kelderak to undertake a heroic journey.

ADLER, BILL, AND THOMAS CHASTAIN
Adler: Born in New York City, 1929; educated at Brooklyn College. He has been an editor at *McCall's* and an editorial director for Playboy Books. Currently a literary agent, he has represented Ronald Reagan, Howard Cosell, Dick Clark, and many other celebrities. He is the author of about 60 books, many of which are nonfiction. Chastain: Born in Nova Scotia but raised in Florida and Georgia. He has worked as a newspaper and magazine writer and editor, and currently is a full-time writer of suspense novels. The two have also coauthored the books *Revenge of the Robins Family* and *The Picture Perfect Murders*. These are both puzzles for readers to solve, but no money was offered for the second one.

Who Killed the Robins Family?   MORROW, 1983
Mystery. The Robins family owns and runs a multi–million-dollar cosmetics company. One by one, eight members of the family are murdered, and the reader must figure out who killed each of them, and how, where, when, and why they died.

A reward was offered for solving the murders, but the contest has since expired.

AGNEW, SPIRO

Born in Baltimore, 1918; educated at Johns Hopkins University and Baltimore Law School. He is a former governor of Maryland, and served as vice-president under Richard Nixon, 1969–1973, until he was forced to resign because of a scandal. He was charged with accepting payments from contractors while governor. An autobiography, *Go Quietly or Else*, was published in 1980.

The Canfield Decision   PLAYBOY PRESS, 1976

American Politics. An ambitious vice-president must contend with intrigue, murder, and Communist agents as he tries for the presidential nomination. But his own private life has problems, too, and someone close to him wants his public disgrace and resignation.

    The novel has some autobiographical components, including attitudes toward the press, the threat of disgrace, and details of the job of vice-president.

AMBLER, ERIC

Born in England, 1909; attended the University of London. He achieved fame as a writer of spy novels in the 1930s with such classics as *Epitaph for a Spy*; *A Coffin for Dimitrios*; and *Journey into Fear*. Later works include *The Intercom Conspiracy* (1969) and *The Care of Time* (1981), his 17th novel. Ambler has also written screenplays (*A Night to Remember*; *The Cruel Sea*) and has published an anthology of spy stories, *To Catch a Spy*, with his own introduction on the nature of spying.

The Levanter   ATHENEUM, 1972

International Intrigue. Michael Howell, engineer and head of the family business, finds himself caught in an agreement with a militant Palestinian action group. Michael, of mixed Middle Eastern heritage himself, must outmaneuver the powerful Palestinian leader Salah Ghaled, people in his own employ, and various government officials, all of whom are carrying on their separate intrigues and deceptions.

    Almost 50 years after his first novel, Ambler creates a very human protagonist and a convincing atmosphere of intrigue.

ARCHER, JEFFREY

Born in England, 1940; educated at the Wellington School and Brasenose College, Oxford. He was the youngest member elected to the House of Commons and served from 1969 to 1974. He has been deputy chairman of the Conservative party since 1985. Besides his three best sellers, he has written *Not a Penny More, Not a Penny Less*; *Shall We Tell the President?* and *A Matter of Honor*.

Kane and Abel   SIMON & SCHUSTER, 1979
  Drama. Chronicles two separate lives from birth into adulthood: one,
  William Kane, a man born to wealth and privilege; and the other, Abel
  Rosnovski, an orphan born to poverty who immigrates to America. William goes to Harvard, is elected to the most exclusive club, and makes
  his first million, while Abel goes to night school, then graduates from
  hotel waiter to assistant manager to owner of the hotel chain. As both
  continue to gain wealth and power, their paths take a collision course.

The Prodigal Daughter   SIMON & SCHUSTER, 1982
  American Politics. Eleven-year-old Florentyna Rosnovski tells her father
  she wants to be president. The story follows her life and early education,
  friends and rivals, and career in politics.

First among Equals   SIMON & SCHUSTER, 1984
  Drama. Traces the lives of three young men, from upper, middle, and
  lower classes respectively, who aspire to be the British prime minister.
  We follow them through three decades of political and personal life
  until one is finally chosen.
      Archer includes background information on British politics and how
  candidates contest for a seat in Parliament.

ARNOLD, ELLIOT
  Born in New York City, 1912. He worked as a reporter for the *Brooklyn
  Times* and the *New York World-Telegram* and served as a captain in the
  air force. He was married and divorced four times. Arnold is also the
  author of *Commandos* and *Blood Brother*. He died in 1980.

A Night of Watching   SCRIBNER, 1967
  War. Within two weeks' time the Danish underground in World War
  II must smuggle 8,000 Jewish refugees to safety in Sweden. A resistance
  leader, a German colonel, a Jewish policeman, and a rabbi all play major
  roles. Many other characters are shown in brief chapters that shift the
  point of view from person to person.
      This is a fictionalized account of an actual event. For the event and
  the author's interviews, see the note at the end of the book.

"ASHE, PENELOPE"
  The pen name of a group of 25 reporters from the Long Island newspaper, *Newsday*, each of whom contributed a chapter.

Naked Came the Stranger   L. STUART, 1969
  Sex. Billy and Gilly, "New York's Sweethearts of the Air," have a popular
  radio talk show. But when Billy starts cheating on Gilly, the show (and
  the marriage, too) is threatened. Gilly decides to get revenge, and do
  some research for the program, by sleeping her way with a series of
  men through the rest of the book. A war-lover, a very modern rabbi,
  a young drug addict, a Mafia lieutenant, and many other colorful characters all come to a bad end after Gilly's attentions.

Intended as a spoof of best-selling novels, the book itself became a best seller. The hoax was discovered after publication.

ASIMOV, ISAAC

Born in Russia, 1920, then moved to New York City at the age of three. He was educated at Columbia University, where he earned a Ph.D. in chemistry and biochemistry. His *Foundation* series, begun in 1951, includes the books *Foundation*; *Foundation and Empire*; *Foundation's Edge*; *Second Foundation*; and *Foundation and Earth* (1986). The series has won a Hugo Award for the Best All-Time Science Fiction Series. While best known for his science-fiction stories, Asimov has also written mysteries, nonfiction books on science and history, and autobiographies (*In Memory Yet Green*; *In Joy Still Felt*). Writing 2,000 to 4,000 words a day, seven days a week, Asimov has produced one book every six weeks for the past 30 years. He believes in the existence of life in other solar systems, does not believe in UFOs, and confesses that he has not flown in an airplane since 1945.

Foundation's Edge   DOUBLEDAY, 1982

Science Fiction. This book continues the *Foundation* series. The Seldon Plan was established to reduce 30,000 years of human misery into only 1,000 years. It called for two colonies of scientists: the First Foundation, composed of a highly publicized group of physical scientists; and the Second Foundation, a secret group of mental scientists. Golan Trevize, of the First Foundation, thinks something is wrong with the plan because it is going too perfectly; so he sets out to find some answers. But Stor Gendibal, of the Second Foundation, is also worried about the plan and begins to follow Trevize. Could there be a third group that has power over them both?

The Robots of Dawn   DOUBLEDAY, 1983

Science Fiction—Mystery. Elijah Baley, police detective from Earth, is called to the planet Aurora to solve a case of apparent roboticide. The "deceased" robot's creator, Earth's future, and Baley's own life depend on his success in solving the case. But as a despised alien, beset by his own personal fears, he finds little support on Aurora. Aided by two robots, he begins his investigation. The case becomes more complicated when Baley discovers that the "dead" robot had served a woman in a rather unique way.

AUCHINCLOSS, LOUIS

Born in New York City, 1917. He was educated at Yale and earned a law degree from the University of Virginia. He is a lawyer on Wall Street and president of the Museum of the City of New York. Among his novels are *Sybil*; *Portrait in Brownstone*; *The Dark Lady*; and *Diary of a Yuppie*. He has also written the autobiographical journal *A Writer's Capital* and a collection of tales called *Skinny Island*.

The Rector of Justin   HOUGHTON MIFFLIN, 1964

Drama. Dr. Frank Prescott is the headmaster of the Justin prep school, in his seventies and eighties for much of the story—self-dramatizing, arrogant, and with great weaknesses. The complex reality of this figure is shown by accounts from his wife, a student he has punished unjustly, a young instructor who worships him, and others.

The Embezzler   HOUGHTON MIFFLIN, 1966

Drama. Guy Prime, once a stockbroker and now in prison, tells of his embezzlement, friendships, and marriage. While Guy is aware of his own limitations, we find out more about him than he himself knows. Then even more is revealed as the story is told from two other points of view.

Tales of Manhattan   HOUGHTON MIFFLIN, 1967

Short Stories. Characters are shown in the drawing rooms, law firms, and art galleries of New York society. In each of the portraits the author lets his characters reveal more about themselves and each other than they know.

A World of Profit   HOUGHTON MIFFLIN, 1968

Drama. Story of the Shallcross family and their friends and associates in the New York financial world. The ambitious Jay Livingston has an impact on each of their lives—as partner, lover, rival, and would-be family member.

The Partners   HOUGHTON MIFFLIN, 1974

Drama. Characters in a law firm are profiled in a series of penetrating sketches. We meet kindhearted Beeky, who has the knack of creating law firms, it seems; Leslie Carter, who always wanted to write a novel—until he found himself put in one; and would-be diplomat Horace Putney, who has a plan for world peace and a wife who organizes undiplomatic parlor games for their Indian and African guests.

AUEL, JEAN M.

Born in Chicago, 1936; educated at Portland State and the University of Portland. She started writing at the age of 40, and has done extensive research for her novels, including visiting prehistoric sites in Europe and learning survival skills. Her Earth's Children series contains *The Clan of the Cave Bear*; *The Valley of Horses*; and *The Mammoth Hunters*, with three more books planned.

The Valley of Horses   CROWN, 1982

Historical Novel–Adventure. Exiled and left to die, young Ayla begins an odyssey to find others like herself. She is a heroine who must learn to survive by her wits, resourcefulness, and skill in healing. Auel creates a strange prehistoric world in this exciting and romantic tale.

BACH, RICHARD

Born in Illinois, 1936; educated at California State at Long Beach. He has been an air force pilot, a charter pilot, and a flight instructor, and owns and flies a biplane. Bach has written about 100 articles on flying, and was the editor of the magazine *Flying*. His other books include *There's No Such Place as Far Away* and *The Bridge across Forever*.

Jonathan Livingston Seagull MACMILLAN, 1970

Drama. This is the story of a seagull who dared to be different from the flock by aiming to perfect his flight. We follow him through several levels of achievement—as student and teacher—as he grows to become a better bird.

Illusions: The Adventures of a Reluctant Messiah DELACORTE, 1977

Religion. In the spirit of *Jonathan Livingston Seagull*, Bach again uses flight to symbolize the attainment of goals. In this story his characters are two men who meet flying their biplanes. One is a reluctant messiah and the other his prospective student.

BACHMAN, RICHARD. See KING, STEPHEN.

BALDWIN, JAMES

Born in Harlem, 1924, to a father who was a preacher. In 1948 he began a 10-year exile in Europe, where he started to write. His political essays—*Notes of a Native Son* (1955), *Nobody Knows My Name* (1961), and *The Fire Next Time* (1963)—made him an intellectual spokesman for the American civil-rights movement. His novels include *Go Tell It on the Mountain*; *Another Country*; and *Just above My Head*. He has also written plays and two recent nonfiction works, *The Price of a Ticket* and *The Evidence of Things Not Seen*, an essay on the Atlanta child murders. He died in 1987.

Tell Me How Long the Train's Been Gone DIAL, 1968

Drama. After a heart attack, Leo Proudhammer, a famous black actor, reflects on his past life. He thinks about his boyhood in Harlem, his ties to his brother Caleb, and the friends he makes as he proceeds with his career in show business. All the while, he tries to discover who he is and how he fits into the world.

BARTH, JOHN

Born in Maryland, 1930. He was educated at Johns Hopkins University, where he later taught creative writing; he played the drums in a neighborhood jazz band, and briefly attended the Juilliard School of Music. He likes to experiment with the novel, and has written such books as *The Floating Opera*; *The End of the Road*; *Lost in the Funhouse*; and *The Tidewater Tales*. He won a National Book Award for *Chimera*.

Giles Goat-Boy DOUBLEDAY, 1966

Science Fiction. Metaphorical fantasy of a world called University run by a computer—WESAC—which is so out of control it must be reprogrammed. George Giles, brought up among goats with no human companionship, is selected to do the job. Giles contends with the computer and with human authorities, but becomes a scapegoat and is sent back to the site of his childhood.

BECKER, STEPHEN
Born in New York State, 1927; educated at Harvard and Yenching University in Peking. Becker has lived in both China and France. He has written fiction and nonfiction, including *Comic Art in America*, and has translated books from the French.

A Covenant with Death   ATHENEUM, 1965
Drama. The story is told by Judge Benjamin Morales Lewis, looking back to the time when he was 29. When a man is accused of murder, the young judge must decide the case. Immersed in his personal conflicts, he begins to ask questions about life and the nature of society. His own life changes as the trial proceeds.

BEHN, NOEL
Born in Chicago, 1928; educated at the University of Wyoming and Stanford University. He served as a field agent in the army's Counter-Intelligence Corps. He has worked as an off-Broadway producer and founded the Musical and Dramatic Theater Academy in New York. Behn left the theater in 1964 to begin writing. *The Kremlin Letter* was his first novel. He has also written *Seven Silent Men*.

The Kremlin Letter   SIMON & SCHUSTER, 1966
Spy. An American intelligence agency must recover a letter that contains an agreement for a cold-war detente. Charles Rone, an ex-Naval Intelligence officer, is trained for the mission, aided by a sadistic chief, a professional pimp, a transvestite, and others. Rone likes money and danger much more than people, but he may not be nasty enough to contend with either his coworkers or his enemies.

BELLOW, SAUL
Born in Canada 1915, and raised in Chicago; educated at the University of Chicago and Northwestern University. Bellow has won National Book Awards for *The Adventures of Augie March*; *Herzog*; and *Mr. Sammler's Planet*, and was awarded the Nobel Prize for Literature in 1976. He is also the author of *More Die of Heartbreak*, which was published in 1987.

Herzog   VIKING, 1964
Drama. The novel begins as Herzog's wife divorces him to live with his best friend. Herzog then writes a series of letters to people living and dead (Nietzsche, Eisenhower, his mistresses . . .) about matters that concern him. He also plans to murder his ex-wife and friend, but fails in this as he has failed in other things. Through the letters and flashbacks, we gain a sense of Herzog's mental turmoil and great physical energy.

Mr. Sammler's Planet   VIKING, 1970
Drama. Artur Sammler has read in the history of civilization, survived the Nazi camps, and known Keynes and H. G. Wells. Now past 70, with

one good eye, he watches a Manhattan pickpocket, interacts with family and friends, and speculates about the continued existence of human life on the planet.

Humboldt's Gift   VIKING, 1975

Drama. Chronicle of Charlie Citrine, a young man with literary ambitions who arrives in Greenwich Village and becomes a disciple of the poet Von Humboldt Fleisher. Charlie faces difficulties with his marriage, his girlfriend, a crook by the name of Ronald Cantabile, and the crook's wife, who is writing a dissertation on Fleisher.

The Dean's December   HARPER & ROW, 1982

Drama. A tale of two cultures. An American dean, Albert Corde, accompanies his wife to Communist Rumania to visit her dying mother. He sees the repressive rule of dictatorship at an immediate and personal level. But he is kept aware of the storm raging at home through his articles on crime, violence, and urban blight. *Corde* means "string" in French, and the dean must try to put together, or at least juxtapose, the two diverse worlds.

BENCHLEY, PETER

Born in New York City, 1940; educated at Harvard. He has traveled around the world, and worked as a reporter for the *Washington Post*, a radio-television editor for *Newsweek*, and a speechwriter for Lyndon Johnson. Benchley's interest in marine biology led him to write about sharks and the ocean, and his novels are based on some scientific fact. He is also the author of *The Island*; *The Girl of the Sea of Cortez*; and *"Q" Clearance*.

Jaws   DOUBLEDAY, 1974

Horror–Adventure. When a young girl is killed by a Great White Shark, the peace of the resort community of Amity is shattered. Sheriff Brody faces major decisions when he must weigh the welfare of the town against the possibility of further shark attacks. Benchley draws on his own experience to show his characters' different views. Hooper, an ichthyologist, sees the beauty in sharks, while the sea captain Quint hates them and sees them as "dumb garbage buckets."

The Deep   DOUBLEDAY, 1976

Adventure. A couple honeymooning in Bermuda hope to find treasure by diving down to wrecks. They find something worth more than gold, however, and an evil native would kill to get it from them. Aided by Treece, the keeper of the lighthouse, soon they care only about getting out of Bermuda alive.

BLATTY, WILLIAM PETER

Born in New York City, 1928; educated at Georgetown University and George Washington University. He was a first lieutenant in the air force from 1951 to 1954, and was a public-relations director at Loyola University. Blatty is a film producer as well as a writer. He produced the film version of his book *The Exorcist*, and won an Oscar in 1973 for the screenplay.

The Exorcist   HARPER & ROW, 1971

Horror–Religion. A little girl in contemporary America is possessed by an evil demon, and a battle is initiated between a priest and the demon for her life. With its carefully drawn characters and detail on possession and the rite of exorcism, this is no ordinary horror story.

BRADFORD, BARBARA TAYLOR

Born in England, 1933; educated in private schools. She has worked as a reporter and columnist in London, and as a syndicated columnist in the United States. Bradford is the author of several interior-decorating books and the novels *A Woman of Substance*; *Hold the Dream*; and *Act of Will*.

Voice of the Heart   DOUBLEDAY, 1983

Glamour. During a production of *Wuthering Heights*, Francesca, a member of English nobility, falls in love with the producer and becomes friends with Katherine Tempest, the beautiful film star. But Katherine betrays them both, and so their lives change course, until they must face each other 20 years later. The romances and tribulations of the characters take us from England to Austria, and then to Hollywood and New York.

BRADFORD, RICHARD

Born in Chicago, 1932; educated at Tulane University and New Mexico State University. He was an editor for the New Mexico Tourist Bureau, a research analyst for the New Mexico Department of Development, and a screenwriter for Universal Pictures. He has also written *So Far from Heaven*.

Red Sky at Morning   LIPPINCOTT, 1968

Drama. When Josh Arnold's father joins the navy in World War II, Josh and his mother are sent to live in New Mexico until the war is over. This is a story about growing up and human relationships, with the pros and cons of the various characters shown in a humorous light.

BRESLIN, JIMMY

Born in Jamaica, New York, 1929; educated at Long Island University. He has written fiction and nonfiction books, and worked as a newspaper columnist. Breslin has visited Ireland several times and makes his home in Queens. He published *Table Money* in 1986 and *He Got Hungry and Forgot His Manners* in 1988.

The Gang That Couldn't Shoot Straight   VIKING, 1969

Drama. A humorous view of organized crime in New York City. Baccala, a big crime boss, has his hands full with a dissident group of Reform Italians headed by Kid Sally. He plans a big bike race for Kid Sally to run, hoping to keep him from causing trouble. But when it fails and the Kid's pride is hurt, the Reform Italians plan to kill Baccala. However, they cannot even put the right ammunition into a gun!

World without End, Amen   VIKING, 1973

Drama. Dermot Davey is failing in his job as a cop and in his marriage. So when the chance comes to visit Ireland he takes it, but he finds more violence and bloodshed in Ulster than he left on the streets of New York.

BRISTOW, GWEN

Born in South Carolina, 1903; educated at Judson College and Columbia. A reporter for the New Orleans *Times-Picayune*, Bristow was best known for her historical fiction (*Jubilee Trail*; *This Side of Glory*). She also wrote mystery novels with her husband. She died in 1980.

Calico Palace   CROWELL, 1970

Historical Novel. Nineteen-year-old Kendra goes alone to live in San Francisco at the height of the California Gold Rush. She marries twice, finds some gold herself, and helps her best friend, Marny, run the Calico Palace, San Francisco's first elegant gambling hall. Life is hard in this new land, and people need a lot of courage.

Teenage or younger readers might enjoy this book.

BUCK, PEARL

Born in West Virginia, 1892, but raised in China, where her parents were missionaries. She attended school at Randolph-Macon and Cornell and became a missionary and teacher in China herself. She won a Pulitzer Prize for her novel *The Good Earth* in 1931 and a Nobel Prize for Literature in 1938. She wrote many other novels, children's books, and essays and the autobiographies *My Several Worlds* and *A Bridge for Passing*. She died in 1973.

The Time Is Noon   JOHN DAY CO., 1966

Drama. Joan Richards returns to her small east Pennsylvania town and bravely endures a life of suffering. She nurses her mother, sees the weaknesses of her father, and goes through an unhappy love affair. When in desperation she finally marries a local farmer, her miseries really begin.

Buck wrote the book 30 years earlier and was advised to withhold it by her publisher-husband.

The Three Daughters of Madame Liang   JOHN DAY CO., 1969

Drama. Madame Liang sees the conflict between the new China and the old and maintains her faith in the Chinese people. She keeps her elegant restaurant to the highest standards of taste, despite official Communist rule, and yet she sends her three daughters to be educated in America. They, too, with their husbands and lovers, must decide what China means to them.

BUCKLEY, WILLIAM F., JR.

Born in New York City, 1925; he was educated at Yale and worked with the CIA in Mexico. He hosted TV's "Firing Line" from 1966. Buckley is editor in chief at the *National Review*, writes a syndicated newspaper column, and lectures widely on politics. He is also the author of *High Jinx* and *Mongoose R.I.P.* (1987).

Saving the Queen   DOUBLEDAY, 1976

Spy. A young American, Blackford Oakes, rich, handsome, and right out of Yale, is recruited to work for the CIA. When he is sent to London to investigate the leak of atomic secrets to the Soviet Union, his job leads him to the private quarters of Windsor Castle and an affair with the young queen of England.

Stained Glass   DOUBLEDAY, 1978

Spy. In the 1950s young Count Axel Wintergrin has a plan to unify Germany under his leadership. When the CIA sends Blackford Oakes to Germany to see what the count is up to, Blackie befriends him. But things become complicated when both the United States and Russia realize that Axel will start World War III. There is no other choice but to eliminate him, and Blackford Oakes is selected for the job.

Who's on First   DOUBLEDAY, 1980

Spy. It's Blackford Oakes again, a little more grown up than when he was saving the queen. Blackie must kidnap a Soviet physicist to keep the American advantage in the space race, but events take a different turn. Buckley adds his own witty comments with caricatures of such figures as Eisenhower, Allen Dulles, and Dean Acheson.

Marco Polo, if You Can   DOUBLEDAY, 1982

Spy. Blackie Oakes, CIA hero, must find out who is leaking information to the Russians from the National Security Council. He is asked to fly a U-2 plane into the Soviet Union and fake a forced landing, allowing a packet of forged documents to fall into enemy hands. Eisenhower, Dulles, and others appear in the story.

An actual incident involving a U-2 plane in the Eisenhower administration was considered a major U.S. blunder. Maybe, Buckley suggests, it was a well-calculated maneuver instead.

The Story of Henri Tod   DOUBLEDAY, 1984

Spy. More complex than Buckley's earlier stories. In 1961, at the height of the Cold War, Blackford Oakes is dispatched to Berlin to contact an anti-Communist leader by the name of Henri Tod. But Tod has a story, too, rooted in 20 years of German history, that can affect the fortunes of the free world. Kennedy, Khrushchev, and Ulbricht are also characters, and the Kennedy stream-of-consciousness passages are worth reading in their own right.

CALDWELL, (JANET) TAYLOR

Born in England, 1900, and raised in the United States. She was educated at the University of Buffalo, and was a yeomanette in the U.S.

Naval Reserve from 1918 to 1919, and a member of the American
Legion. She was married four times. From *Dynasty of Death* (1938) to
Answer as a Man (1981), Caldwell published a novel regularly every year
or every second year for a total of 32 books. She died in 1985.

A Pillar of Iron   DOUBLEDAY, 1965
Historical Novel. Cicero is the pillar of iron in this tale of the last days
of the Roman democracy. Caldwell traces his life from youth and early
education through a career as a lawyer and statesman to his final years
and philosophical writings. Other historical figures—Julius Caesar, Bru-
tus, Sulla, Scaevola—also make appearances.

Testimony of Two Men   DOUBLEDAY, 1968
Historical Novel. A Victorian doctor, Jonathan Ferrier, has been accused
of killing his wife by an abortion but has been acquitted by the court.
Embittered by the scandal, he trains a young successor and plans to
leave town. He has made powerful enemies, however, by fighting hy-
pocrisy and incompetence, and these people have even more malice in
mind.

Great Lion of God   DOUBLEDAY, 1970
Historical Novel–Religion. Caldwell gives an account of Saint Paul before his conversion to Christianity, focusing on his childhood and early
adult years. Saul, as he was then called, was born to a well-to-do Jewish
family in Rome. He grew up torn by his own strong emotions and sense
of sin, and was gifted as a soldier and scholar.

About half of the book is devoted to statements of philosophy and
descriptions of Roman life and customs.

Captains and the Kings   DOUBLEDAY, 1972
Historical Novel–Saga–American Politics. This is the story of the Irish
Armagh family, from their arrival as immigrants to the time a son runs
for president of the United States. Young Joseph comes to America and
rises through his own hard work and shrewdness to amass great wealth.
He is also helped by his willingness to work on both sides of the law.
He goes on to become a powerful force in politics and dreams of his
son becoming the first Catholic president. But is there a curse on the
family? And will it spare his son Rory, already elected senator and on
his way to the White House?

Caldwell says in the preface that she knows of no real family like
the Armaghs.

Ceremony of the Innocent   DOUBLEDAY, 1976
Historical Novel–American Politics. Ellen Watson, a servant girl, is suddenly thrust into a Cinderella world of riches when she marries Jeremy
Porter. But Ellen, like America itself on the eve of World War I, is
unable to recognize the evil around her. If Jeremy dies, Ellen will lose
her protector and the country will lose the one voice warning of conspiracies that seek to plunge the nation into war.

Bright Flows the River   DOUBLEDAY, 1978
Drama. Guy Jerald has come to hate his affluent life, his marriage, and
his two very unlikable children. He attempts suicide, will not speak to

anyone for weeks after, and is institutionalized by his family. As James Meyer, an old friend and psychiatrist, talks to him, both men must decide what to do with their lives.

Throughout the book Caldwell advances her own critical opinions of society and human nature.

Answer as a Man   PUTNAM, 1980

Historical Novel–Religion. Jason Garrity rises from poverty to become part owner of a resort hotel. But his principles and faith are tested by the unscrupulous people around him and by tragedies and betrayals in his own family.

CASSILL, R. V. (RONALD VERLIN)

Born in Iowa, 1919; educated at the University of Iowa, where he later taught creative writing. In addition to his many novels (*The Goss Women*; *Hoyt's Child*; *Labors of Love*, among others), he has written criticism, essays, and short stories under his own name and his pen name, Owen Aherne.

Doctor Cobb's Game   BERNARD GEIS, 1970

Drama–Sex. Michael Cobb, medical doctor and dabbler in occult practices, is accused of giving classified British information to foreign powers. As the novel proceeds, we are told more about how he did this, why people put up with his sadism, and why they jump to do his bidding. Espionage is only incidental to this story of strong sexual motivation and strange relationships.

CHEEVER, JOHN

Born in Massachusetts, 1912. After he was expelled from Thayer Academy "for smoking and laziness," his short story "Expelled" appeared in the *New Republic* when he was 18. His work received critical praise from the beginning. Altogether, he has written over 100 short stories and several novels, including *The Wapshot Chronicle*, winner of the 1957 National Book Award, and *The Wapshot Scandal*. A novella, *Oh What a Paradise It Seems*, was published in 1982. He died in 1982 after a long bout with cancer.

Bullet Park   KNOPF, 1969

Drama. A satiric look at affluent society where the trivial is juxtaposed with the important. It is the story of the people who live in the town of Bullet Park, particularly Eliot Nailles, his son Tony, and Paul Hammer, a newcomer who threatens the Nailleses' pleasant existence.

Falconer   KNOPF, 1977

Drama. A view of prison life and the life outside by Ezekiel Farragut, an ex–college professor unjustly charged with killing his brother. Through the brutality and loneliness of prison, Farragut keeps his capacity for thought and feelings, and in the face of death wins back his life.

The Stories of John Cheever   KNOPF, 1978

Short Stories. This collection contains over 60 stories written between 1946 and 1978 and published in the *New Yorker*, *Playboy*, *Esquire*, and the *Saturday Evening Post*. Some of the stories, for example "The Country Husband," "The Enormous Radio," and "The Swimmer," have appeared in several anthologies. The stories provide a panoramic view of Cheever's writings, showing glimpses beneath the surface of men, women, and children in different situations of life. In the Preface, Cheever writes, "The Constants . . . are a love of light and a determination to trace some moral chain of being."

CHRISTIE, (DAME) AGATHA

Born in Torquay, England, 1890; educated at home and then in private schools. She worked as a hospital dispenser in World War I and, after the failure of her first marriage, married an archaeologist. Christie wrote her first detective novel in 1920, and went on to write a total of 95 books which have sold over 500 million copies. She often used the same sleuths in several novels, including Hercule Poirot, Miss Jane Marple, and Tommy and Tuppence Beresford. In addition, she wrote the play *The Mousetrap*, which has run for more than 30 years in London. She died in 1976.

Passenger to Frankfurt   DODD, MEAD, 1970

Suspense. When a strange request is made to Sir Stafford Nye by an unfamiliar girl in an airport, he willingly complies. He sees her again when his help is needed once more, this time by a "board of inquiry" whose purpose is to collect information on groups who are trying to change the world through violence.

The authors of *The Agatha Christie Companion* (Delacorte Press, New York, 1984) agree with other critics who call this book "one of her worst."

Nemesis   DODD, MEAD, 1971

Mystery. A man leaves Miss Jane Marple a generous legacy in his will, providing that she can solve a certain crime. There is a catch, however, for he does not tell her anything about the crime! She accepts the challenge, and clues begin to appear as she takes a coach tour and visits with three sisters. Then she learns how deadly "love" can be.

Postern of Fate   DODD, MEAD, 1973

Mystery–Spy. Tommy and Tuppence Beresford, Agatha's crime-fighting couple, are now in their seventies and have just bought a house. When they move in, they find clues to a murder that occurred over 60 years before. They start investigating it for fun, but soon realize that someone does not want them probing into the past.

Curtain   DODD, MEAD, 1975

Mystery. Hercule Poirot's health is declining rapidly; this will be his last case. He insists that his old friend Captain Hastings come to see him at Styles, the house where they first met years ago. Poirot claims that a crime will be committed there and that he needs Hastings's help to prevent it. The strange part about it, however, is that Poirot tells him very little, only showing him newspaper clippings about four apparently unrelated murders.

This novel was actually written in the 1940s.

Sleeping Murder   DODD, MEAD, 1976
Mystery. Vague but terrifying childhood memories are awakened when young Gwenda Reed buys a house in England. Was someone close to her murdered there 18 years before? Miss Jean Marple helps Gwenda and her husband solve the mystery, but first warns them to "let sleeping murder lie."

This was Christie's last novel to be published before her death, but, like *Curtain*, it was written in the 1940s.

CLANCY, TOM

Born in 1947. He worked as an insurance broker in Maryland until he published his book *The Hunt for Red October*. President Reagan and members of the White House staff liked the book so much that Clancy was invited for a private chat with the president and lunch with the staff. He has since written *Red Storm Rising* and *Patriot Games*.

The Hunt for Red October   NAVAL INSTITUTE PRESS, 1984
International Intrigue. A Russian navy officer decides to defect to the United States and take his nuclear submarine with him. The sub is subsequently pursued by both American and Russian ships. Clancy shows the action on all the various ships and also contrasts the wonders of American capitalism (supermarkets, cable TV) with Russian repression. He incorporates research on American and Soviet military strategy and submarine technology. The U.S. Navy cooperated with the author of this very patriotic book.

CLARKE, ARTHUR CHARLES

Born in England, 1917; educated at King's College and the University of London. He served in the RAF as a radar instructor from 1941 to 1946. Clarke is an expert on technology, particularly aeronautics. His fiction includes *Childhood's End* (1953), *The Nine Billion Names of God* (1967), *2001: A Space Odyssey* (1968), and *The Songs of Distant Earth* (1986). He also writes nonfiction works about space travel.

2010: Odyssey Two   NEW AMERICAN LIBRARY, 1982
Science Fiction. This is the continuation of the story told in *2001*. The United States sends the *Discovery II* to Jupiter to investigate the monolith phenomenon and try to reactivate the Hal 9000 computer. However, the Soviets are there, too; so the two countries join together in a semi-cooperative mission and discover the function of the monolith.

CLAVELL, JAMES

Born in Australia, 1924, the son of Sir Richard and Lady Ross Clavell. He was educated at Birmingham University, and served as a captain in the Royal Artillery from 1941 to 1946. While in service, he was captured by the Japanese and spent three years in POW camps, where the conditions were so harsh that only 10,000 of the 150,000 prisoners survived. Clavell was the executive producer of *Shōgun* for TV, which earned him an Emmy in 1981. He wrote the screenplays for *The Fly* (1956); *Squadron*; *The Satan Bug*; and *The Great Escape*, which won the Writers Guild Award. His first novel, *King Rat*, was based on his prisoner-of-war experience. He has also written *The Children's Story*; *Thump-O-Moto*; and *Whirlwind*.

Tai-Pan   ATHENEUM, 1966

Historical Novel–Adventure. In the 1840s Britain takes possession of the island of Hong Kong, and the Opium Wars begin. Dirk Struan, Scotsman and owner of the Noble House trading company, is called Tai-Pan—supreme ruler—by the Chinese. He realizes the importance of Hong Kong for trade with Britain, so he and his vast fleet haul anything they can, particularly opium and tea. But both manmade and natural conflicts plague Struan, and in Tyler Brock, the owner of another trading company, he finds a very formidable opponent.

Shōgun   ATHENEUM, 1975

Historical Novel–Adventure. In the 17th century John Blackthorne, an English sea pilot, is stranded in feudal Japan with his life at stake. He does not understand the ways of the Japanese, and the Catholic priests who interpret for him try to show him as an enemy. He finds his place, however, when he meets Toranaga, a feudal lord who desires ultimate power—he wants to be Shōgun—and insists that Blackthorne is to help. Romance is also present when the Lady Mariko falls in love with Blackthorne. She is a Catholic convert torn by conflicting loyalties to the church and her country.

The story is based loosely on the life of the historical figure Will Adams, an English sailor who became a retainer to one moving to power within Japan.

Noble House   DELACORTE, 1981

Drama–Spy. In 1963, the Noble House is still the largest trading company on Hong Kong, and its new Tai-Pan is Ian Dunross. Clavell gives us the details of only 10 days of action; yet in that time we see bank runs, stock-market changes, a deadly fire, a natural disaster, horse racing, world politics, and an intricate spy network. As we follow Dunross's struggles to maintain the Noble House in its top position, a wide assortment of other characters come into the action, including various spies, policemen, and a host of Asians whose family histories are always explained.

At 1,206 pages, this is the longest of the listed best sellers.

COLLINS, JACKIE

She is a resident of London and the sister of actress Joan Collins. Jackie gave up her own show-business career to work as a novelist. Among other books, she has written *Lovers and Gamblers*; *The Bitch*; *Hollywood Husbands*; and *Rock Star*.

Hollywood Wives   SIMON & SCHUSTER, 1983
Glamour–Sex. In Hollywood, three couples pursue lives of success, sex, and status. Shoplifter Elaine is married to a fading actor, innocent Angel has a gigolo for a husband, and scriptwriter Montana's husband plays the field. Meanwhile, a detective is pursuing a disturbed young murderer. Soon the lives of all these characters interconnect and lead to a violent conclusion.

COLLINS, LARRY, AND DOMINIQUE LAPIERRE
Collins: Born in Connecticut, 1929; educated at Loomis Institution and Yale. He worked as a Middle Eastern correspondent from 1957 to 1959, and as Middle Eastern editor for *Newsweek* from 1959 to 1961. Other novels include *O, Jerusalem!*; *Freedom at Midnight*; and *Fall from Grace*. Lapierre: Born 1931. He is a French novelist and nonfiction writer, and the former editor of *Paris Match*.

The Fifth Horseman   SIMON & SCHUSTER, 1980
International Intrigue. Suppose Colonel Qaddafi smuggled a nuclear bomb into New York City to be exploded if the United States did not agree to his demands? What follows is a very detailed account of events that could occur—in the White House, in New York, and in intelligence centers around the world. There are no real characters in the novel, just page-long scenes describing various people and the actions they take as the three-day countdown begins.

COOK, ROBIN
Born in New York City, 1940; educated at Wesleyan and the College of Physicians and Surgeons, Columbia University. He lives in Boston, where he is a practicing ophthalmologist and teacher at the Harvard Medical School. In addition to his fiction, he has written scientific articles and the nonfiction book *The Year of the Intern*. A recent novel, *Outbreak*, was followed by *Mortal Fear*.

Coma   LITTLE, BROWN, 1977
Mystery. Something is wrong at Boston Memorial Hospital as patients admitted for routine operations never return from the operating table. When young medical student Susan Wheeler begins to investigate, she finds her career and then her life in jeopardy.

Brain   PUTNAM, 1981
Mystery. This time something is wrong at Hobson University Medical Center. One patient died on the operating table and had her brain secretly removed. Others have exhibited strange mental breakdowns and bizarre behavior. Martin Philips and Denise Sanger, doctors and lovers, risk their careers and lives to find the answer.

Godplayer   PUTNAM, 1983

Mystery. Cassi, a young medical student and diabetic, is worried about her own health and the fact that her famous surgeon-husband is taking drugs. Meanwhile, someone is killing the terminal patients at Cassi's hospital—and *she* may become the next victim.

CRAVEN, MARGARET

Born in Montana, 1901; she spent her early years at Puget Sound, Washington, and graduated from Stanford University. From the 1940s to the 1960s she published numerous short stories that have been translated into several languages and collected in *The Home Front* (1981). She died in 1980.

I Heard the Owl Call My Name   DOUBLEDAY, 1973

Religion–Drama. A dying young vicar is sent by his Bishop to live with a small Indian village in the Northwest, in the hope that they will all receive some benefit from the situation. In the short time that the vicar spends there, he learns what life is about and of the sadness of the Indians who are losing their children to the cities.

CRICHTON, MICHAEL (PRONOUNCED CRY-TON)

Born in Chicago, 1942; educated at Harvard, where he obtained a medical degree and wrote his first novel. He also directs films, including the production of his own book *The Great Train Robbery*, and Robin Cook's best seller *Coma*. His novel *Sphere* appeared in 1987.

The Andromeda Strain   KNOPF, 1969

Suspense. An organism escapes in a bacteriological warfare project, killing everyone in a small Arizona town. A team of scientists and a doctor are dispatched to isolate the organism and stop its spread. The story is presented as if it were fact, with liberal doses of scientific information (maps, computer readouts, technical memos) supplied to add authenticity.

The Terminal Man   KNOPF, 1972

Suspense. Harry Benson, computer scientist, has electrodes implanted in his brain to cure his periods of blackouts and violence. A sympathetic doctor, Janet Ross, tries to help, but Harry escapes the hospital and a human time bomb is released.

Crichton supplies details on electrical stimulation of the brain and includes an annotated bibliography.

The Great Train Robbery   KNOPF, 1975

Historical Novel. In 1855, a train is robbed of 12,000 pounds of gold bullion. The story explains how Edward Pierce planned and executed the robbery, and follows through to his ultimate trial. Other people who were involved as accomplices, some unknowingly, are also depicted. Many historical details of the period are given.

CRICHTON, ROBERT (PRONOUNCED CRY-TON)

Born in New Mexico, 1925; educated at Harvard. He served in the army during World War II. Crichton is also the author of *The Great Imposter* and *The Rascal and the Road*, both works of nonfiction.

The Secret of Santa Vittoria　　　　　　　　SIMON & SCHUSTER, 1966

War. During World War II, the inhabitants of the Italian town of Santa Vittoria must try to protect their one million bottles of wine from the Nazis. After many disasters, the townspeople, led by their rather comic mayor, Italo Bombolini, do outwit the Germans and Captain Sepp Von Prum. Comedy, the barbarism of war, and symbolism are combined in this unusual tale.

The Camerons　　　　　　　　　　　　　　　KNOPF, 1972

Historical Novel. In turn-of-the-century Scotland, young Maggie Drum leaves the coal-mining town of Pitmungo to capture a husband. She snares Gillon Cameron, a poor Highlander, and takes him back to Pitmungo to work in the mines. Maggie runs the family and has big plans for the future, forcing them to put their earnings into the family kist. But larger issues loom in their lives as the miners are exploited and one son studies socialist theories. Finally, Gillon Cameron takes charge of his life and family and threatens Maggie's lifelong dream.

CUSSLER, CLIVE

Born in Illinois, 1931, and grew up in Alhambra, California; educated at San Jose State. He enlisted in the air force during the Korean War, worked as a creative director in advertising agencies, and began writing in 1965. Like his hero Dirk Pitt, Cussler collects classic automobiles and has led expeditions in search of famous shipwrecks.

Deep Six　　　　　　　　　　　　　　　SIMON & SCHUSTER, 1984

International Intrigue–American Politics. A powerful Asian shipping enterprise has hijacked a ship with the U.S. president on board; their purpose—to sell the president to the Russians for a diabolical mind-control experiment. The crisis builds when the newly brainwashed president returns home, announcing his peace plans with the Russians. In the meantime, hero Dirk Pitt must find a sunken ship filled with deadly nerve gas and rescue a congresswoman who has been kidnapped from another ship by the Asians.

DAVIS, GWEN

Born in Pittsburgh, 1936; educated at Bryn Mawr and Stanford University. Her novel *Touching* (1971) is based on her experience in therapy, which resulted in a legal suit against her and a major court case. She is also the author of *Naked in Babylon*; *Sweet William*; and *Silk Lady*, and has written poetry and screenplays.

The Pretenders　　　　　　　　　　　　WORLD PUBLISHING, 1969

Glamour–Sex–Drama. A satiric look at the lives of some Beautiful People of the 1960s where only the surface counts and money and recognition are the sole values. There is Diane, who does everything (too perfectly) that people tell her to; Andre, whose aspirations far outrun his abilities; and Maggie, who is so rich that people will not admit that she is insane. Finally, there is Louise, who would like to join the charmed circle but must first decide the price she is willing to pay.

DE BORCHGRAVE, ARNAUD, AND ROBERT MOSS

de Borchgrave: Born in Belgium, 1926. He has been a chief foreign correspondent and senior editor for *Newsweek* and received the Overseas Press Club's Prize in 1971 for best magazine reporting from abroad. He is currently editor in chief of the *Washington Times*. Moss: Born in Australia, 1946. He has been an editor for *Foreign Report*, a publication of the London *Economist*. Moss has written articles for magazines and books of fiction and nonfiction. The novel *Moscow Rules* was published in 1985.

The Spike   CROWN, 1980

International Intrigue. The Russians have infiltrated American government agencies and newsrooms, feeding innocent reporters "disinformation" (lies that have some of the veneer of truth). Robert Hockney, who has made his reputation by investigating the CIA, has been the unwitting dupe of this disinformation. When he discovers the size of the conspiracy, he must try to ensure that his story is not suppressed. But this will be difficult because KGB agents have infiltrated all of the government—there are 171 agents in the White House alone!

DE HARTOG, IAN (JAN)

Born in Holland, 1914; he ran off to sea when he was still young. His book *Holland's Glory* (1940) about Dutch oceangoing tugboats was banned by the Nazis, although it never mentioned the war or the Germans. During the war, de Hartog escaped to England, a trip that took six months. In this time he was imprisoned several times, crashed in a plane, and was wounded. His fiction includes *The Call of the Sea*; *The Little Ark*; and *The Commodore* (1986). He won a Tony Award in 1952 for his screenplay *The Fourposter* and has written mysteries under the name of F. R. Eckmar.

The Captain   ATHENEUM, 1966

War. The story of how a young Dutchman, Harinxma, became captain of an oceangoing tugboat and how he and his crew—all civilians—were assigned to serve a British convoy in World War II. De Hartog's knowledge of boats combines with insights into individual character and the relationships between captain and crew.

DEIGHTON, LEN

Born in London, 1929; attended the Royal College of Art in London. He worked as a journalist and authored two books on World War II (*Blitzkrieg*; *Fighter*) before turning to fiction in the 1960s. He spends time in the United States, but makes his home in Ireland with his wife and children. Among his many thrillers are *The Ipcress File*; *XPD*; and *London Match*. *Winter* appeared in 1988.

Funeral in Berlin   PUTNAM, 1965

Spy. A very professional British agent attempts to smuggle a Russian scientist out of East Berlin with the help of a Russian security officer. If readers lose the plot through all the double and triple crosses, they can rejoin Deighton for an exciting conclusion.

The Billion Dollar Brain   PUTNAM, 1966

Spy. A British agent is assigned to infiltrate a computer-based espionage organization run by the extreme reactionary General Midwinter. The assignment takes him to Helsinki, Riga, and San Antonio, where the Brain is located. He must also deal with stolen viral samples, a defection to Russia, and a beautiful female assassin.

SS-GB   KNOPF, 1979

Mystery–Spy–War. Imagine that England has been occupied by the Nazis in World War II. The king is imprisoned in the Tower, and the SS is in charge of Scotland Yard. Detective Superintendent Douglas Archer is working on a routine murder case, but is soon led into the thick of English resistance efforts and a search for information that may decide the outcome of the war. As the plot becomes increasingly complex, Archer does not know who his friends and betrayers are or whether his actions will help to save—or kill—the king.

Berlin Game   KNOPF, 1984

Spy. Moscow has buried an agent at the highest levels of British intelligence, someone who has been working there for years. To trap the traitor, senior agent Bernard Sampson must begin to put the pieces together, evade the traps, and arrange a split-second escape. He knows it must be one of his closest friends or fellow workers.

DELDERFIELD, R. F. (RONALD FREDERICK)

Born in London, 1912. He served in the RAF from 1940 to 1945 as a public-relations officer in Europe. For a time he worked on the staff of his father's country newspaper, and he then turned to the writing of plays. From 1950 to 1970 he wrote histories and novels about English life. His books include *A Horseman Riding By*; *The Green Gauntlet*; *Too Few for Drums*; and *Return Journey*. He died in 1972.

God Is an Englishman   SIMON & SCHUSTER, 1970

Historical Novel–Saga. In 1857 Adam Swann returns from the Crimea to establish an empire of freight-hauling coaches and to marry the daughter of the local mill owner. Together, the couple meet some unexpected windfalls and misfortunes. The book portrays England in a changing era and the details of London and country life.

Theirs Was the Kingdom   SIMON & SCHUSTER, 1971

Historical Novel–Saga. This book continues the story of the Swann family from the years 1878 to 1889. The lives of Adam Swann's many children provide a panoramic view of life in Victoria's England. Alex fights the Zulu warriors; Stella makes a disastrous marriage to an upper-class homosexual; rambunctious George gets involved in his father's business and the new horseless carriages; and adopted daughter Deborah crusades against white slavery.

This is volume 2 of the saga. The third and final volume is *Give Us This Day* (1973).

To Serve Them All My Days   SIMON & SCHUSTER, 1972

Drama. The setting is England between the two world wars. Recovering from a wound and the trauma of World War I, David (PJ) Powlett-Jones begins to teach in a public boys' school. The years pass, with some tragedy, escapades, and accomplishment, and PJ becomes headmaster as England enters World War II.

DICKEY, JAMES LAFAYETTE

Born in Georgia, 1923; educated at Vanderbilt University and served in the air force. He is a former athlete and teacher and has written advertising copy for Coca Cola, Lay's Potato Chips, and Delta Airlines. Primarily a poet, Dickey has written many volumes of verse and commentary. His first novel, *Deliverance*, was followed by *Alnilam* in 1987.

Deliverance   HOUGHTON MIFFLIN, 1970

Adventure. What begins as a weekend canoe trip for four men quickly turns into a nightmare of survival when they are set upon by murderous, perverse locals. If they are to get out of the wilderness alive, they must come to terms with their own fears and learn the cunning of killers.

DIDION, JOAN

Born in California, 1934; educated at the University of California at Berkeley. She has written fiction and nonfiction, including the novel *Play It As It Lays* (1970) and the acclaimed nonfiction book *Slouching towards Bethlehem* (1968).

A Book of Common Prayer   SIMON & SCHUSTER, 1977

Drama. The story of Charlotte Douglas, a 40-year-old Californian, as told by a 60-year-old American woman living in Boca Grande. Charlotte, who has recently suffered a nervous breakdown, is searching for her daughter,who joined a radical group engaged in bombing and hijacking. Despite two bad marriages, her daughter's disappearance, and other trials, Charlotte still believes things will work out—right to the final events in the story.

DOCTOROW, E. L.

Born in New York City, 1931; educated at Kenyon College and Columbia University, and served in the army from 1953 to 1955. Doctorow worked as an editor in book publishing until he began to write full-time. His first novel was *Welcome to Hard Times* (1960). He has also written *The Book of Daniel*; *Lives of the Poets*; and *World's Fair*.

Ragtime RANDOM HOUSE, 1975

Historical Novel. A critical look at America in the early 20th century, from the immigrants to the wealthy. Real and fictional characters are portrayed, from Harry Houdini, J. P. Morgan, Emma Goldman, and Booker T. Washington, to a father, mother, and little boy. At the heart of the action is a black musician who demands compensation and then revenge for incidents involving racial prejudice.

Loon Lake RANDOM HOUSE, 1980

Drama. In the Depression of the 1930s, young Joe of Paterson, N. J., runs away from home and comes upon Loon Lake, a steel tycoon's magnificent estate in the Adirondacks. The satire mixes narrative and stream of consciousness as Joe journeys back to become master of Loon Lake.

DONALDSON, STEPHEN REEDER

Born in Ohio, 1947; educated at the College of Wooster and Kent State. He is the winner of several science-fiction awards, including the John W. Campbell Award for best new writer at the World Science Fiction Convention in 1979. His three-volume series the Chronicles of Thomas Covenant was followed by three more books in the Second Chronicles of Thomas Covenant. Another series called Mordant's Need consists of the books *The Mirror of Her Dreams* (1986) and *A Man Rides Through* (1987).

The One Tree BALLANTINE, 1982

Science fiction. Covenant and Linden go in quest of the One Tree to save the Land from the Sunbane and Lord Foul. Accompanied by strange beings, they sail on a great ship crewed by the gregarious Giants, and meet other dangerous and mysterious creatures. Plagued with self-doubt from past experiences, both Thomas and Linden have problems confronting the dangers they are subjected to.

This is Book Two in the Second Chronicles, and although it may be read alone, it is advisable to read the preceding books first to gather the full meaning of the continuing story.

White Gold Wielder BALLANTINE, 1983

Science Fiction. In this conclusion to the Chronicles, Covenant and Linden return to the Land in one last hope of saving it. During their travels they are reacquainted with old friends and face old and new enemies. Questions are answered and secrets are revealed when the company finally confronts Lord Foul with the White Gold power.

DRURY, ALLEN

Born in Texas, 1918; educated at Stanford University and served in the army from 1942 to 1943. He worked as a Washington correspondent for the *New York Times* and *Reader's Digest*. His first political novel, *Advise and Consent*, won a Pulitzer Prize in 1959. He has also written *The Hill of Summer* (1981) and *Pentagon* (1986).

Capable of Honor   DOUBLEDAY, 1966

American Politics. The author imagines an all-powerful news columnist, Walter Dobius, who can make and break presidential candidates and whose word is law to the rest of the media. Dobius interacts with characters already familiar to Drury readers—Secretary of State Orrin Knox, Governor Ted Jason, and President Harley Hudson. Intrigue and violence follow in the selection of the next presidential and vice-presidential nominees.

Preserve and Protect   DOUBLEDAY, 1968

American Politics. The president, already nominated for a second term, has been killed, and 106 members of the National Committee must pick a new nominee. Intrigue, corruption, and arguments about foreign policy follow, mixed with riots, violence, and the storming of the convention. Which of the clearly opposed candidates will be nominated? And what will happen then?

The Throne of Saturn   DOUBLEDAY, 1971

American Politics. The space program encounters conflict with the Russians and a race problem at home. The decision to launch a space probe to Mars is opposed by the liberal press, a union leader (who is a Communist in disguise), and others. Soon the president finds himself pressured to accept a black astronaut on the crew and to invite the Soviets to join the mission. Problems increase as sabotage occurs at the test site, hatred erupts during the flight, and the mission meets a hostile Soviet ship in space.

Come Nineveh, Come Tyre   DOUBLEDAY, 1973

American Politics. A sequence of violent events finds Ted Jason, the liberal governor from California, elected president. Meanwhile, the United States is still trying to quell Communism by military involvement in Gorotoland and Panama. Protest groups want the nation out of war, and so more violence breaks out at home.

Promise of Joy   DOUBLEDAY, 1975

American Politics. A war between China and Russia threatens the world. Can the determined American president find a way out and still continue to resist the Communist drive for world dominion? There is conflict at home, too, and all the continual crises that Drury readers have come to expect.

DU MAURIER, (DAME) DAPHNE

Born in London, 1907; educated in Paris. Many of her novels and period romances are set in the West Country, where she lived much of her life. Her novel *Rebecca* (1938) brought her worldwide fame, and was followed by *My Cousin Rachel*. She died in 1988.

The Flight of the Falcon   DOUBLEDAY, 1965

Mystery. Armino Fabbio, a courier for a tour company, suddenly finds himself connected to the murder of a peasant woman in Rome. When he returns to his home town of Ruffano to discover why the woman died, he uncovers some of his own family secrets too. He is haunted by memories of his older brother Aldo, shot down in flames in World War II, and by the legend of the infamous Duke Claudio. When a festival is held to celebrate the flight of Duke Claudio, Armino realizes how frightening the outcome could be.

The House on the Strand   DOUBLEDAY, 1969

Historical Novel. In modern England, a man is lent a house by a professor friend, but in return he is to serve as a guinea pig for a drug. When he takes the drug, England as he knows it disappears, and he finds himself in the 14th century. Subsequent "trips" find him more involved with the people and politics of the time, and soon he is bored with his actual world. Can he control his use of the drug? And are the trips imaginary or real?

DURRELL, LAWRENCE GEORGE

Born in India, 1912. He moved to England in his late teens, and lived a large part of his life in the eastern Mediterranean, which forms the background for much of his writing. Durrell published poetry and prose at a young age and went on to achieve fame with the Alexandria Quartet, consisting of four novels: *Justine*, *Balthazar*, *Mountolive*, and *Clea*. He has also published several volumes of collected poems. A sequel to *Tunc* is the novel *Numquam*, published in 1970.

Tunc   DUTTON, 1968

Drama–Science Fiction. Inventor Felix Charlock is hired by the firm of Merlyn and marries the strange Benedicta, who promptly leaves him. His employer remains a voice on the telephone, his friends disappear mysteriously, and a loaded revolver is placed in his office. Along with the present-day action, Durrell plays off the past and future. Charlock's friends have the names of the ancient muses, but his computer can tell the future. Events move from the Acropolis to a brothel in Athens to a futuristic all-seeing "firm." *Tunc* is Latin for "then" or "next" in an orderly sequence; however, Durrell suggests that reality may not possess that kind of order.

ECO, UMBERTO

Born in northern Italy, 1932; educated at the University of Turin with a Ph.D. in 1954. He is now a professor of semiotics at the University of Bologna, with several of his scholarly books available in English translation. He has also written *The Bond Affair*, which studies the cultural significance of James Bond, and a collection of essays entitled *Travels in Hyperreality*.

The Name of the Rose   HARCOURT, 1983

Mystery–Historical Novel–Religion. The book is at the same time a mystery, complete with murders, a trail of clues, and the unique detective Brother William of Baskerville; a display of philosophical argument from Aristotle to Bacon; and a richly detailed historical account of the life and intrigues of 14th-century Italy. These are combined in a tale that moves with devastating logic to a conclusion readers must appreciate for themselves.

First published in Italian in 1980. The film version does not do justice to the novel.

EDEN, DOROTHY

Born in New Zealand, 1912. She has written some three dozen books of historical fiction and Gothic romance, including *The Millionaire's Daughter*; *Speak to Me of Love*; and *The Time of the Dragon*. She died in 1982.

The Vines of Yarrabee   COWARD, MCCANN, 1969

Historical Novel. A picture of 19th-century Australia in a time of passion and struggle. To this land comes young, aristocratic Eugenia in an arranged marriage with a man obsessed with making wine at Yarrabee. Their lives—and the compromises they make with the land and each other—are the subject of the story.

ELEGANT, ROBERT

Born in New York City, 1928; educated at Pennsylvania, Yale, and Columbia, earning a master's degree in Chinese and Japanese. He has lived in Hong Kong, Tokyo, Singapore, and Ireland, and worked as a foreign correspondent with syndicated columns in the United States and abroad. He has also published nonfiction books on Asia, and the novel *From a Far Land*.

Dynasty   MCGRAW, 1977

Saga. Life in Hong Kong from the turn of the century to the 1970s. Young Mary Osgood from England arrives in Hong Kong, where she marries into the Sekloons, the merchant princes of the island who have developed a huge trading empire. Mary's family is buffeted by war, plague, and the conflicting political loyalties of two sons. The story concludes when the family is again united to celebrate the matriarchal Mary's 90th birthday.

EPHRON, NORA

Born in New York City, 1941, to parents who were film writers and producers; educated at Wellesley. She has worked as a freelance writer and a contributing editor and columnist for *Esquire* and *New York* magazines. Her divorce from *Washington Post* journalist and writer Carl Bernstein forms the background to *Heartburn*.

Heartburn   KNOPF, 1983

Drama. Rachel, seven months pregnant and 38 years old, finds her husband is unfaithful. Frightened and hurt, she tells us about her life, friends, family, and cookbook recipes. Then she makes a decision.

ERDMAN, PAUL

Born in Ontario, 1932; educated at Georgetown University, with a Ph.D. from the University of Basel in Switzerland. A banker and economist, he was imprisoned in Switzerland after being charged with an illegal financial deal. There he wrote *The Billion Dollar Sure Thing*. He has recently written *The Panic of '89* and *The Palace* and has published books of investment advice.

The Billion Dollar Sure Thing   SCRIBNER, 1973

International Intrigue. Foreign-exchange rates, intrigue, and personal status engage a cast of characters including Swiss bankers, Russians, a safecracker, and an American financial genius who works for the Arabs. Watch for Comrade Melekov, the Russian yuppie with his designer tie and plans for an Oldsmobile Ninety-Eight.

The Crash of '79   SIMON & SCHUSTER, 1976

International Intrigue. Banker Bill Hitchcock, 44, has made enough money to retire when the Saudis ask him to become their financial adviser. Accepting the challenge for fun, Hitchcock wheels and deals with the world's richest and most powerful. But a logical chain of events soon pushes things out of control. We find out why the Saudi defense buildup occurred, why the Swiss atomic scientist helped, and why the United States joined in to contribute to its own collapse.

The Last Days of America   SIMON & SCHUSTER, 1981

International Intrigue. Erdman has the uncanny ability to make his plots sound like next year's headlines. Frank Rogers, the president of a California aerospace company, goes to Europe to secure a multi–billion-dollar missile deal. But suddenly he finds himself the target of banks, the West German government, and the Swiss police. Meanwhile, the events he has helped set in motion change the balance of world power.

FAIRBAIRN, ANN (PSEUDONYM OF DOROTHY TAIT)

Born in 1902(?). An American journalist and novelist, she also wrote *That Man Cartwright* and *Call Him George*. She died in 1972.

Five Smooth Stones   CROWN, 1966

Drama. David Champlin, a black, rises from poverty to attend Harvard Law School and Oxford and become a leader in the civil-rights movement. He is a cerebral hero, thoughtful and wary, analyzing himself and the motives of others. In his choice of work and love for a white woman, he tries to remain true to himself. The title refers to the biblical David, who faced a Goliath with only a slingshot and five smooth stones.

FAST, HOWARD

Born in New York City, 1914; attended the National Academy of Design, and served in the Office of War Information during World War II. Fast is best known as a writer of historical fiction, with books on the American Revolution and the four-volume series listed below. He was a member of the Communist party from 1943 to 1956 and, like his heroine in *The Establishment*, was questioned by the House Un-American Activities Committee and went to prison briefly. *The Naked God* (1957) is an account of his Communist experience. He has also written short stories, plays, biographies, children's books, and, under the pen name E. V. Cunningham, detective stories. Novels include *Max* and *The Immigrant's Daughter*, the conclusion to the Lavette saga.

The Immigrants   HOUGHTON-MIFFLIN, 1977

Saga—Historical Novel. The son of immigrants, Dan Lavette rises from rags to riches in early 20th-century San Francisco. Starting with only a small fishing boat, he makes thousands of dollars in a few days ferrying people from the devastation of the San Francisco Earthquake. The book follows Dan and his partner and their friends and families as they build a vast shipping empire. Along the way, Dan has a ruined marriage and falls in love with a Chinese feminist. The book ends in the Depression of the 1930s.

Second Generation   HOUGHTON-MIFFLIN, 1978

Saga. The children of Dan Lavette take very different paths as they become adults. Barbara, the main character in the continuing Lavette story, participates in a San Francisco strike, helps run a union soup kitchen, becomes a successful writer, and falls in love. Her brother Tom, joining with their mother's second husband in his search for wealth and power, takes over the Selden Bank. Meanwhile, father Dan begins to build ships for the approaching war.

The Establishment   HOUGHTON-MIFFLIN, 1979

Saga. Third in the series of books on the Lavette family. The time is 1948. Barbara's husband is called on a secret mission to help the Israelis, while she must undergo the harassment and injustice of the McCarthy investigations taking place in Congress. We also watch her unscrupulous brother Tom in his drive for power, as well as her sister-in-law's career as a Hollywood star.

The Legacy   HOUGHTON-MIFFLIN, 1981

Saga. The story of the Lavettes continues through the events of the 1960s. Barbara writes a book, gets a divorce, and organizes Mothers for Peace. Her son Sam goes to Israel to find out who he is and becomes involved in the Six-Day War. Other third-generation Lavettes face prejudice, a civil-rights lynching in the South, and conflict in Vietnam.

FLEMING, IAN

Born in England, 1908; educated at Eton and Sandhurst and then began work as a journalist. He was in the Royal Naval Volunteer Reserve from 1939 to 1945, worked in the secret service, and served as assistant director of Naval Intelligence. He became renowned as the creator of the James Bond character, and wrote more than a dozen Bond adventures from the 1950s until his death in 1964. Titles include *Casino Royale*; *Diamonds Are Forever*; *Goldfinger*; and *On Her Majesty's Secret Service*.

You Only Live Twice NEW AMERICAN LIBRARY, 1964

Spy. After suffering a personal tragedy, James Bond blunders two missions, and M. at Headquarters is worried that his best man can no longer do his job. Instead of asking for his resignation, he strips him of his "oo" license to kill and sends him on a diplomatic mission to Japan. But the mission soon leads to a series of tests and a confrontation with the evil Dr. Shatterhand.

The Man with the Golden Gun NEW AMERICAN LIBRARY, 1965

Spy. The action starts immediately in this story. After being missing for a year and presumed dead, James Bond suddenly appears at Headquarters, brainwashed by the KGB. Bond is assigned a mission: if he accomplishes it, all will be forgiven; but if he fails, well, it is better than serving 20 years for what he does while brainwashed. His foe, however, is not easy. He is Scaramanga, and when he aims his golden gun, he does not miss.

FOLLETT, KEN

Born in Cardiff, Wales, 1949; educated at the University of London. He worked as a reporter and then became a publishing executive. His book *Eye of the Needle* won the Edgar Award of the Mystery Writers of America. *Paper Money,* written before *Eye of the Needle*, was reissued in 1987.

Eye of the Needle ARBOR HOUSE, 1978

War–Spy. For the success of the Normandy Invasion, the Allies must fool the Germans into believing the landing will take place elsewhere— at Pas de Calais. One German spy is in a position to know that the Pas de Calais landing is fake. As all Britain hunts him, he meets up with a courageous woman on a lonely Scottish coast. Her actions may decide the outcome of the war.

Triple ARBOR HOUSE, 1979

Spy. When Israeli intelligence learns that Egypt is building a nuclear reactor in the West Desert, they decide that Israel must obtain uranium to make its own bombs. Nat Dickstein, a survivor of the concentration camps and the Israelis' prime agent, must plan a way to steal 200 tons of uranium without anyone knowing that it is missing. But when Dickstein encounters people he used to know at Oxford, his mission and his life are jeopardized.

The Key to Rebecca MORROW, 1980

War–Spy. Two men must try to outwit each other during Rommel's 1942 campaign against the British. One is master spy Alex Wolff, part German and part Arabian, who holds the key to Rebecca; and the other is British agent William Vandam, who must catch Wolff and risk his own son's life in the process. We see the skills, mistakes, and humanity of the two antagonists.

The Man from St. Petersburg   MORROW, 1982

Historical Novel–Spy. In the last days before World War I, a British earl and a Russian prince conduct secret negotiations for an alliance. But another Russian enters the picture—to assassinate the prince and convulse the earl's family with secrets from the past. Follett supplies fully drawn characters and some good detail on the tensions in British society at the time.

FORSYTH, FREDERICK

Born in England, 1938. He served as a Royal Air Force fighter pilot and then worked as a foreign correspondent until 1969. He has traveled to more than 40 countries and speaks several languages. Tired of journalism, he sat down on January 1, 1970, and wrote *The Day of the Jackal* in 35 days and nights.

The Day of the Jackal   VIKING, 1971

International Intrigue. An extremist French organization plots to kill De Gaulle and needs an assassin not known to any police force. They pick the Jackal, a gentlemanly English professional killer, who is the best in his field. Against him are mobilized the security forces of seven countries and Claude Lebel, deputy chief of the Paris police. Lebel is the best in his field, too, and he must find and stop the Jackal with almost no information to begin with. Along with the detail on these two unique characters, Forsyth gives us a close look at Paris at the time.

Forsyth got the idea for the story while working in Paris during the attempt to assassinate De Gaulle. The assassination attempt is historical fact; the rest is fiction.

The Odessa File   VIKING, 1972

Spy. A reporter gets possession of an old man's diary that tells of the actions and subsequent escape of Nazi war criminal Edvard Roschman. The reporter sets out to bring Roschman to justice and infiltrates ODESSA, the secret society that is aiding and protecting former SS agents. The novel is set primarily in Germany in 1963.

The Dogs of War   VIKING, 1974

International Intrigue. A British mining company discovers valuable platinum in an unstable African country and plots to claim it for themselves. They hire a mercenary soldier, keeping him blind to their real purpose, which is to kill the present leader so that they can insert a man of their choice. The mercenary hires others to help him and begins to purchase the tools of his trade. When these details are finally completed, the strike is on.

The Devil's Alternative   VIKING, 1979

Spy. The failure of Russia's grain crop forces the Kremlin into steps toward a peace treaty with the United States. But a Ukrainian nationalist is fighting his own war against the Kremlin, and the repercussions take the world to the brink of nuclear war. Forsyth brings us a host of well-drawn characters and an unusual love story. In fact, the bond between a British agent and a Russian stenographer may be the only way to avert war.

The Fourth Protocol   VIKING, 1984

Spy. Russian agents plot to destabilize Britain and bring the Radical Left to power. British agent John Preston must fight through his own bureaucracy to stop the Russians, but several other unique characters—on both sides of the Iron Curtain—are doing their own plotting too.

FOWLES, JOHN

Born in England, 1926; educated at the Bedford School and New College, Oxford. Fowles worked as a schoolteacher before becoming a full-time writer. He lives in an 18th-century villa overlooking the English Channel and pursues his hobbies as a naturalist and collector. "I get much more pleasure from writing than from being published," he remarked in a Book-of-the-Month Club interview. "I like the creation of another world." His first novel, *The Collector*, was published in 1963.

The French Lieutenant's Woman   LITTLE, BROWN, 1969

Historical Novel. Writing from a 20th-century point of view, Fowles makes Victorian England come alive in its manners, philosophies, and details of daily life. Charles Smithson, outwardly scientific and cynical but at heart a romantic, is smitten with Sarah Woodruff—"the French Lieutenant's Woman"—who keeps her own secret in the midst of the scandal that surrounds her.

The Ebony Tower   LITTLE, BROWN, 1974

Short Stories. Five stories that Fowles calls variations on themes in earlier books. Mysteries are posed, love is glimpsed or rejected, passion breaks through simple domestic lives.

Daniel Martin   LITTLE, BROWN, 1977

Drama. Daniel Martin is called back to England to visit his dying friend Anthony. The two friends are married to sisters, but Daniel knows that he has married the wrong sister, and he discovers that Jane (Anthony's wife), too, has married the wrong man. The mystery of these relationships is posed at the beginning of the story, with pieces of the puzzle supplied as the book goes on. All the while, Fowles gives us commentary on life in both the 1950s and the 1970s in England and America.

FRANCIS, DICK

Born in South Wales, 1920; he left school at the age of 15, and served in the RAF from 1940 to 1945. A former steeplechase jockey, he rode in 2,305 races, winning many. Francis then wrote a racing column for London's *Sunday Express*. He has been writing thrillers for about 25 years, and all of them have something to do with horses. Some titles are *Flying Finish*; *In the Frame*; *Risk*; and *Bolt*. He has also written the recent biography *A Jockey's Life: The Biography of Lester Piggott*. When asked whether he would rather talk about books or horses, he said, "Horses anyday. . . . Books are hard work" (p. 221, Polak, *The Writer as Celebrity*).

Reflex PUTNAM, 1981

Mystery. Philip Nore, steeplechase jockey and amateur photographer, is told that his dying grandmother wants him to search for a sister he never knew he had. At the same time, Philip comes to the aid of a fellow jockey whose photographer father has just been killed in an accident. But when Philip finds some of the dead man's photographs, he realizes that he has evidence that could ruin many people and cost him his life.

Twice Shy PUTNAM, 1982

Suspense. Jonathan Derry, a young physics teacher and expert marksman, is given three computer tapes from a friend in danger. The tapes, containing a horse-racing betting system, soon lead Jonathan and his wife into danger, too. Fourteen years later, his brother William is confronted about the tapes. He must learn their history—and find out where they are—to protect himself and put an end to their misuse.

FREEMAN, CYNTHIA (PSEUDONYM OF BEA FEINBERG)

Born in New York City. She was educated in public schools and then worked as an interior designer. She is also the author of *A World Full of Strangers*; *Catch the Gentle Dawn*; and *Illusions of Love*.

Portraits ARBOR HOUSE, 1979

Saga. The story of Sarah and Joseph, Jewish immigrants to America, and their children and grandchildren. This family portrait focuses on personal problems and relationships. One generation affects the next, as parents who in childhood were unwanted and unloved pass on the scars to their own children.

Come Pour the Wine ARBOR HOUSE, 1980

Drama. A woman's process of self-discovery is traced from age 19 through marriage, motherhood, and divorce, culminating in a romance at age 45.

No Time for Tears ARBOR HOUSE, 1981

Saga. The story follows Chevala Landau and her family from turn-of-the-century Russia to the founding of the state of Israel in 1948.Fleeing a pogrom against Jews, the family moves to Palestine and then to America. Among other events, the husband, Dovid, joins fellow Israelis in spying for Britain during World War I; Chevala rises to become head of a large jewelry empire in New York; and her sister, who has married a German, is threatened at the coming of the Third Reich.

FRENCH, MARILYN

Born in New York City, 1929; educated at Hofstra College with a Ph.D. from Harvard. She is the author of *Her Mother's Daughter* (1987) and has written a book on James Joyce and many scholarly articles.

The Women's Room SUMMIT BOOKS, 1977

Sex–Drama. The story tells the history of several women from the 1950s to the beginning of the 1970s, showing their marriages, life changes, and growth of a new awareness. Often eloquent and unsparing in its account of ordinary events, the book is one of the strongest expressions of feminist thinking among the best sellers.

The Bleeding Heart   RANDOM HOUSE, 1980
Sex–Drama. Investigation of a love affair between Dolores, a professor on fellowship in England, and Victor, with a wife at home in Scarsdale who has tried to commit suicide. Dolores is outraged at the suffering that women are subject to, and yet she finds herself the Other Woman in the affair. She helps Victor gain a new understanding of his wife, and she wins a temporary victory with herself. Nevertheless, the author does not let her readers escape from facing what is, essentially, a grim situation.

GAINHAM, SARAH (PSEUDONYM OF RACHEL AMES)
Born in London, 1922. She has written for the *Spectator* and other British and American publications, and has worked as a broadcaster for the BBC and for West German and Austrian television. She has written five previous novels and currently lives in Vienna.

Night Falls on the City   HOLT, RINEHART, & WINSTON, 1967
War. The action takes place in Nazi-occupied Vienna from 1938 to 1945. Julia, a famous stage actress, must play her most challenging role by continuing her career while hiding her Jewish husband from the Gestapo. The war, however, takes its toll on their lives. The setting shows the author's knowledge of Vienna and research on the history of the time.

A Place in the Country   HOLT, RINEHART, & WINSTON, 1969
War. A detailed picture of postwar Vienna, where the aftermath of war brings suspicion, guilt, and fear. In this sequel to *Night Falls on the City*, actress Julia Homburg, her ward Lali, and Georg Kerenyi try to pick up the pieces of their lives, and a new character is added, the young British soldier and narrator Robert Inglis.

GALBRAITH, JOHN KENNETH
Born in Canada, 1908; Ph.D. from Harvard. Galbraith is a well-known economist and author of the nonfiction books *The Affluent Society* and *The New Industrial State*. He served as ambassador to India in the Kennedy administration. He has recently published *A View from the Stands*.

The Triumph   HOUGHTON-MIFFLIN, 1968
American Politics. Witty satire about how foreign policy is made in the State Department. A revolution is occurring in a Latin American dictatorship, against the wishes of bureaucrats of the United States. We follow the tired ambassador, the old-guard assistant secretaries, and the ousted dictator, complete with his private wealth and mistresses, through to the ironic conclusion. Readers will find many details here that only an insider could know.

GANN, ERNEST

Born in Nebraska, 1910; educated at Yale. He served as a pilot in the Army Air Transport Command from 1942 to 1946, attaining the rank of captain. He wrote the novel and the screenplay for *The High and the Mighty* (1953) and many other screenplays. He has also written an autobiography, *A Hostage to Fortune* (1978), and the novel *The Triumph*.

The Antagonists   SIMON & SCHUSTER, 1970

War–Historical Novel. In the first century A.D. the Romans are completing the conquest of Judea, except for one group of Jews entrenched on the Masada rock. General Flavius Silva and Eleazar ben Yair are the antagonists who find they have more in common with each other than they do with their own people. Silva's campaign is complicated also by his love for a Jewish captive, the strong and spirited Sheva. The story, based on a historical event, shows the military strategy and human weaknesses of both sides.

GARDNER, JOHN CHAMPLIN

Born in Batavia, New York, 1933; educated at Washington University, St. Louis, with a Ph.D. from the University of Iowa. He taught medieval literature and creative writing at several universities and wrote fairy tales, books on Chaucer, and criticism of modern fiction. Novels include *Freddy's Book* and *Michelsson's Ghosts*, as well as *Grendel*, a story of *Beowulf*'s monster, written as a sympathetic account from the monster's point of view. His *October Light* won the National Book Critics Circle Award. He died in 1982.

The Sunlight Dialogues   KNOPF, 1972

Drama. Fred Clumly, police chief of Batavia, New York, believes in law and order and solid traditional virtues. The Sunlight Man (actually Taggart Hodge, originally from Batavia) believes in magic, violence, and individual freedom. When Taggart escapes from jail, Clumly must hunt him down. Complex in structure, the book combines real-world violence, Arthurian symbolism, and a picture of Middle America in the late 1960s.

Nickel Mountain   KNOPF, 1973

Drama. Henry Soames, the fat owner of a truck-route diner in the Catskills, marries pregnant 16-year-old Callie out of kindness. Through loss and disappointment, the family survives and Henry keeps his dignity. Other characters, too, see their hopes destroyed and do the best they can.

The book is subtitled *A Pastoral Novel*. Etchings are by Thomas O'Donoghue.

October Light   KNOPF, 1976

Drama. Conflict breaks out between brother and sister as 72-year-old James locks his 80-year-old sister in the upstairs bedroom. Soon Sally does not want to come out, despite the attempts of relatives and friends to persuade her. Conservative and liberal attitudes also clash: farmer

James looks back to the time of Ethan Allen and thinks the country is going to hell, while Sally believes in New York City and amnesty. It is not until the end of the novel that a resolution is reached, bringing the old man a profound revelation about tragedies of the past.

GARDNER, JOHN EDMUND

Born in England, 1926; educated at St. John's College, Cambridge. He was ordained a priest in the Church of England and left the priesthood to become a theatre critic and art editor. Best known as a writer of suspense fiction, Gardner wrote *The Liquidator* (1964) as a deliberate parody of the James Bond stories. When the publishers were looking for a writer to continue the Bond series 14 years after Ian Fleming's last novel, they turned to him. Other Bond stories include *License Renewed* (1981), *Icebreaker* (1983), *Role of Honor* (1984), and *No Deals, Mr. Bond* (1987). Gardner has also written the novels *Flamingo* (1983) and *The Secret Generations* (1985).

For Special Services   COWARD, MCCANN, & GEOGHEGAN, 1982
Spy. Changes have occurred over the years in the British Secret Service, including the disbanding of the Double-O Section, but James Bond is still the potent secret agent. When a rash of recent hijackings is linked to SPECTRE, Bond, together with the daughter of his old friend Felix, must investigate. They are led to the superluxurious ranch of Bismaquer, with its maximum security, while, unknown to Bond, an old enemy is trying to eliminate him once and for all.

GILDEN, K. B. (PSEUDONYM OF HUSBAND AND WIFE KATYA AND BERT GILDEN)

Katya was born in Maine, no date supplied, and educated at Radcliffe; Bert was born in 1915 and died in 1971. The two collaborated on short stories, screenplays, and another novel, *Between the Hills and the Sea* (1971).

Hurry Sundown   DOUBLEDAY, 1964
Drama. A long (1,000+ pp.) but lively narrative of a southern town in the days of change after World War Il. Progress is coming to Colfax County, Georgia, along with a sense of rising expectations and new conflict between the races. Interlocking narratives follow several characters closely and show the spirit of the place and time: the black and white soldiers who had been childhood friends; the ruthless new entrepreneurs, and the old forces of hate and bigotry.

GODDEN, RUMER

Born in Sussex City, England, 1907; she spent much of her childhood in India. She has written novels, short stories, and children's books. Her best seller is based on information she gathered while living at the gates of a Benedictine monastery in England.

In This House of Brede   VIKING, 1969
Religion. The story of Philippa, who enters a convent at the age of 40, and of the other nuns and life in the convent itself.

GODEY, JOHN (PSEUDONYM OF MORTON FREEDGOOD)
Born in New York City, 1912; he has lived in four of the city's boroughs. Some of his novels are *The Gun and Mr. Smith*; *The Man in Question*; *This Year's Death*; and *The Clay Assassin*. He has also published stories in magazines.

The Taking of Pelham One Two Three   PUTNAM, 1973
Suspense. Four desperate men take over a subway train and hold the passengers hostage. The story is told from a constantly changing point of view, including those of the four men, a hooker, the mayor, and policemen. Godey gives an in-depth look at his characters and how they are motivated by their jobs, sex, race, and innermost fears.

GOLD, HERBERT
Born in Cleveland, 1924; educated at Columbia and the Sorbonne. He has written more than 20 books and numerous short stories and essays published in leading magazines. His novels include *The Optimist*; *Therefore Be Bold*; *A Girl of Forty*; and *Dreaming*.

Fathers   RANDOM HOUSE, 1966
Saga. Told as a son's memoir of his father. The story follows Sam Gold through his life from his emigration from Russia at the age of 13 until he is an old man in the 1960s and his son is a father, too. In this largely autobiographical work, the author gives a close look at what it means to be a father.

GORDON, NOAH
Born in Massachusetts, 1926; educated at Boston University, where he earned a master's degree in English. He served in the army from 1945 to 1946, and worked as a reporter for the Boston *Herald*. *The Rabbi* is his first novel, and he has published articles and short fiction. His most recent book is *The Physician* (1986).

The Rabbi   MCGRAW, 1965
Religion. The career and conflicts of Rabbi Michael Kind as told by the 45-year-old rabbi himself. He reviews his service with various congregations and suffers with his wife (a convert to Judaism) in her mental breakdown. His struggle proceeds through doubt and bitterness to a new hope in the strength and future of the Jewish faith.

GOUDGE, ELIZABETH (PRONOUNCED "GOOZH")
Born in England, 1900. She wrote short stories, children's books, and adult fiction, including *Green Dolphin Street* (1944), which became a film. Her autobiography, *Joy of the Snow*, was published in 1974. She died in 1984.

The Child from the Sea COWARD, MCCANN, 1970
Historical Novel. A romantic tale of Lucy Walter, a little-known figure in 17th-century England who was mistress to King Charles I and mother of the Duke of Monmouth. Lucy grew up with trouble in her home and civil war in England. She fell in love with a childhood friend—who became the king of England. In the novel they marry, although secretly; and so begins a life for Lucy of separation from the man she loves, poverty, and unfair damage to her reputation.

GOULD, LOIS
Born in New York City, 1938(?); educated at Wellesley College. She worked as a police reporter, executive editor for *Ladies' Home Journal*, and columnist for the *New York Times*. Some of her books are *Necessary Objects*; *Final Analysis*; and *La Presidenta*, the story of the Argentinian leader Eva Peron.

Such Good Friends RANDOM HOUSE, 1970
Drama–Sex. Maintaining a vigil outside her unfaithful husband's hospital room, Julie Messinger looks back at her life and marriage, and out at the world around her. Wryly comic but uncompromising, Julie shows how one woman attempts to cope with crisis.

GREELEY, ANDREW
Born in Illinois, 1928. Greeley was raised in Chicago, where most of his stories are set and was ordained a Roman Catholic priest in 1954. He went on to receive a Ph.D. from the University of Chicago. Besides being a novelist and a priest, he is a sociologist, a professor, and the author of a syndicated column. He has written over 100 books, both scholarly and popular. Recent works include the autobiographical *Confessions of a Parish Priest*; *Angels of September*; *Patience of a Saint*; *Rite of Spring*; and *Happy Are Those Who Thirst for Justice*.

Thy Brother's Wife WARNER BOOKS, 1982
Religion–American Politics–Sex. Sean, the hero of the story, becomes a priest and, despite his criticism of the church, goes on to become archbishop. His older brother Paul—weak, self-indulgent, and a womanizer—enters politics and wins a seat in Congress. But Sean loves his foster sister Nora, who is Paul's wife. And the skeletons in Paul's closet begin to catch up with him. Interspersed with the adultery, incest, blackmail, suicide, and murder are biblical quotations and discussions of the need for change in the church.

Lord of the Dance WARNER BOOKS, 1984
Religion–Sex. The Irish Farrells of Chicago have fought their way up from poverty to a position of power and wealth. One son is running for governor, and the other, a priest, is a famous TV personality, in love with his brother's wife. But when teenaged heroine Noele decides to trace a family mystery, some terrible secrets come to light. There is

crime, politics, passion, and redemption as the dance unfolds and builds
to a climax.

GREENE, GAEL

Born in Detroit; educated at the University of Michigan. She has worked
as the restaurant critic for *New York* magazine. *Blue Skies, No Candy* is
her first novel. She has also written the nonfiction book *Delicious Sex*
which includes her advice for "more fun in bed or on the kitchen table."

Blue Skies, No Candy   MORROW, 1976
Glamour–Sex. Kate Alexander is 40, with a successful career as a screenwriter and a good marriage. But she embarks on a series of sexual
adventures that culminate in an affair in the glamorous worlds of Paris
and Cannes.

GREENE, (HENRY) GRAHAM

Born in England, 1904; educated at Berkhamsted School, where his
father was headmaster, and at Balliol College, Oxford. He served in
the Foreign Office from 1941 to 1944. He published a book of verse
while in school, and since has made his living as a writer, including jobs
as literary editor on the *Spectator* and *Night and Day*. Some of Greene's
many novels are *The Third Man*; *This Gun for Hire*; *The Power and the
Glory*; and *The Quiet American*. He has also written plays and travel books
and the autobiographical *Ways of Escape* (1980), which describes the
source of many of his novels.

The Comedians   VIKING, 1966
Drama. Misters Brown, Smith, and Jones confront violence and death
in Haiti. Brown is a lapsed Jesuit who runs a tourist hotel; Jones is a
con man and soldier of fortune; and Smith is a vegetarian (who once
ran for president on the Vegetarian ticket) who has come to found a
center for the poor. Brown is the narrator, with an eye for farce and
an understanding of human feeling.

Travels with My Aunt   VIKING, 1969
Drama. Henry Pulling is a bachelor and retired bank manager who
keeps himself busy with his dahlias. But when he meets his elderly but
lively aunt, things begin to change. He travels with his aunt from Europe
to Istanbul to Paraguay, encountering some odd people along the way,
and begins to realize what a boring life he has been leading!

The Honorary Consul   SIMON & SCHUSTER, 1973
International Intrigue–Religion. A doctor, an excommunicated priest,
and a minor British official (the honorary consul) are caught in a bizarre
kidnapping trap. They have all lost fathers, and they do not believe in
God. In a world that seems to have abandoned them, each must work
out his own code of morality and individual honor.

The Human Factor   SIMON & SCHUSTER, 1978
Spy–Drama. Espionage and human drama combine in this story of
intrigue within a British intelligence operation. All of the characters are

rendered in depth, with their own unique personalities. The protagonist is Maurice Castle, on the surface a methodical functionary doing routine work on the African desk, but underneath a man of powerful loves and hates. Then there is also the odd little bookstore owner, a very vulnerable investigator, and Castle's African wife, Sarah.

GRIFFIN, (ARTHUR) GWYN

English author, born 1922. After service in World War II, he traveled widely, never staying long in any one country. He worked briefly as a police officer in the Sudan and ran a pub in England. He is the author of six novels, including *A Last Lamp Burning*; *The Occupying Power*; and *Master of This Vessel*, and a volume of short stories. He died in Italy in 1967.

An Operational Necessity   PUTNAM, 1967

War. A German submarine in World War II sinks a British ship and guns down the lifeboats of the few survivors. The German captain claims it was "an operational necessity" to destroy the evidence that would reveal the submarine's location. Based on historical fact, the book tells of the action, its aftermath, and the final courtroom trial. All of the characters are interesting. Odd, fallible, and often comic, they are forced to face issues of moral responsibility and the justice of life or death.

HABER, JOYCE

Born in New York City, 1932; educated at Barnard. She has worked as a Hollywood columnist and journalist and has written for the *Los Angeles Times* and *Time-Life*. She has also appeared in films and on television and radio.

The Users   DELACORTE, 1976

Glamour–Sex–Drama. A critical inside look at Hollywood society, where everyone uses everyone else in the search for status and success. The action focuses on Elena, a leading Hollywood hostess, who is trying to keep up appearances while trapped in a marriage to a fading star.

HACKETT, GENERAL SIR JOHN

Born in Australia, 1910; educated at New College, Oxford, and the Imperial Defense College. He is a retired British army soldier and a scholar with a number of honorary degrees. He was decorated in World War II and served as commander in chief of the British Army of the Rhine. He currently is a visiting professor in the classics at King's College.

The Third World War: August 1985   MACMILLAN, 1978

War. Written in the format of a history text, as if the events had actually taken place. The authors set the stage for the war as they look at the political and economic instabilities of many countries and what they mean to the Superpowers. Following this is a brief description of the mobilization of forces in Europe, the fighting and the limited nuclear attack, and finally the political and economic results of this brief war. The main thesis throughout is that the West must maintain and build up *conventional* military force if the threat of nuclear holocaust is to be avoided.

Other military personnel collaborated with Hackett on this book.

HAILEY, ARTHUR

Born in England, 1920; he joined the British Royal Air Force at the age of 19 and served as a pilot and flight lieutenant. His success as a writer began with the television drama "Flight into Danger," which became the novel and film *Runway Zero-Eight*. Five best sellers in a row followed. Hailey announced his retirement in 1979, entering a hospital for quadruple-bypass surgery. He felt so good after the surgery, however, that he wrote *Strong Medicine*.

Hotel   DOUBLEDAY, 1965

Drama. Five days with major and minor crises in the life of a grand New Orleans hotel, its employees and guests. Action includes a civil-rights conflict, the doings of a professional hotel thief, and the threat that the hotel will be sold to a chain. Hailey provides information on hotel management, conventions, credit, and security.

Airport   DOUBLEDAY, 1968

Suspense. A series of emergencies at a major international airport. There is a midair collision, a possible bomb on another plane, a community up in arms about noise-abatement procedures, and a furious winter storm. Hailey provides information about airport management and maintenance.

Wheels   DOUBLEDAY, 1971

Drama. There are more personal crises here than industrial ones, although we see the threat of organized crime, worries about a new model car, and a robbery-murder. Information on the auto industry—design, advertising, unions, and even dealerships—is included.

The Money-Changers   DOUBLEDAY, 1975

Drama. Characters in one of the nation's leading financial institutions must deal with counterfeit credit cards, a bank run, a multinational loan scheme, and a dying bank president who will need a successor. We watch the unlikable Roscoe Heyward and the likable Alex Vandervoot compete for the position and learn a lot about the inside workings of the money business.

Overload   DOUBLEDAY, 1979

Drama. A number of emergencies confront Nim Goldman, vice-president of Golden State Power and Light. A terrorist group is bombing generators, while environmentalists protest the building of new power plants. Increased energy demands from the world oil crisis result in brownouts and blackouts. Along with the narrative, Hailey shows the inner workings of a power company and how it relates to people in their private homes and in the world.

Strong Medicine DOUBLEDAY, 1984

Drama. Characters in a drug company must worry about the release and recall of a deadly drug, a Senate investigating committee, the Animal Rescue Army, and work on another drug that might have effects as an aphrodisiac. Information on the politics and economics of drug production is included with the narrative.

HARRIS, THOMAS

Born in Tennessee, 1940(?). He spent his childhood in Mississippi and was educated at Baylor University. He worked his way up from the Waco, Texas, *Tribune-Herald* to become an Associated Press reporter in New York. Harris researched the idea for *Black Sunday* with other reporters and resigned his job to write the book. He has also written *Red Dragon*.

Black Sunday PUTNAM, 1975

International Intrigue. Michael Lander, a disturbed Vietnam veteran attempting to control his rage, decides to join with the Palestinian terrorists to get revenge for crimes against the people. Dahlia Lyad is the highly skilled Arab terrorist who works with him and becomes his lover. Their scheme is to explode 600 kilos of plastic explosives covered with rifle darts at the Superbowl, where the president of the United States will be among the spectators. They will use a blimp, with Lander as pilot, to carry out the mission. But an international group is tracking them down by the trail of murders they are leaving in their wake.

HAWLEY, CAMERON

Born in South Dakota, 1905; educated at South Dakota State. He has worked as an advertising writer and director, has written for television, radio, and film, and has published short stories. He died in 1969.

The Hurricane Years LITTLE, BROWN, 1968

Drama. The hurricane years are the heart-attack years for overpressured middle-aged businessmen. Judd Wilder, director of advertising and promotion for Crouch Carpets, suffers his first attack and gives us a detailed account of his physical and emotional state. He is treated by Dr. Aaron Kharr, who argues throughout the book for the importance of psychological factors in prevention and recuperation. Judd's wife, boss, and rival are also shown.

HAYDEN, STERLING

Born in New Jersey, 1916. He served in the Marines from 1942, and with the OSS until 1946 as a secret agent in Nazi-occupied countries with the rank of captain. He received the Silver Star for Bravery. Hayden has been an actor in many movies, including *The Asphalt Jungle*; *The Godfather*; *Nine to Five*; and the television production *The Blue and the Gray*. He died in 1986.

Voyage: A Novel of 1896   PUTNAM, 1976

Historical Novel. Panoramic view of the shipping industry on the eve of the 20th century and the great contrast between the haves and the have-nots at the time of the American Gilded Age. On New Year's Day 1896, the huge iron-hulled ship *Neptune's Car* begins its voyage hauling coal from Maine to San Francisco. Conditions for the crew are terrible, bringing violence and near-mutiny. At the same time, the shipbuilder's family voyages on a luxurious private yacht to Japan, returning to San Francisco along with *Neptune's Car* at the time of the Bryan-McKinley presidential election.

HELLER, JOSEPH

Born in Brooklyn, 1923; educated at New York University and at Oxford, where he was a Fulbright Scholar. He was a professor of English briefly at City College. Heller served as a bombardier in World War II, and used this experience in his first novel, *Catch 22*.

Something Happened   KNOPF, 1974

Drama. Corporate executive Bob Slocum tells us about himself and how things have gone wrong. Something is wrong with his job, his wife, and his two older children (neither of whom is named). In addition, he has a severely retarded younger son, Derek, whom no one loves. Sex is no longer enjoyable, and he is beset by a multitude of vague fears. When something does happen in the novel, and tragedy strikes, things continue pretty much as they were before. A classic statement of the misery at the heart of a successful American life.

Good as Gold   SIMON & SCHUSTER, 1979

American Politics. Dr. Bruce Gold, professor of literature, has the chance to become a high White House official. So he leaves the book he is writing on "the Jewish Experience," enters Washington life, dates the daughter of an anti-Semite, and considers divorcing his wife. Gold is a thinly disguised Henry Kissinger, and the story satirizes White House politics, Kissinger, bigotry, and Gold's own opportunism.

HEMINGWAY, ERNEST MILLER

Born in Illinois, 1899. He worked as a reporter both in Kansas City and for the *Toronto Star*. He was a volunteer ambulance driver on the Italian front in World War I and was injured, then lived in Paris among the American expatriate literary group. Hemingway was also a war correspondent in World War II, and lived in Cuba briefly, where he learned deep-sea fishing. This passion led to his novel *The Old Man and the Sea*. Among his other well-known books are *The Sun Also Rises*; *Death in the Afternoon*; and *To Have and Have Not*. He was awarded the Nobel Prize for Literature in 1954. He committed suicide in 1961 after a long illness.

Islands in the Stream   SCRIBNER, 1970

War. The novel is divided into three parts, each one an important episode in the life of Thomas Hudson, a painter. It begins with "Bimini" in the 1930s, where Thomas entertains his three sons from two marriages. In "Cuba" in 1942, he is involved in the war against Germany and also encounters his first wife. The book is concluded "At Sea," where Hudson pursues survivors from a German U-Boat.

Published nine years after Hemingway's death and edited by Mary Hemingway and the publisher.

HERBERT, FRANK

Born in Tacoma, Washington, 1920. Herbert worked as a newspaperman in several cities on the West Coast and spent 10 years with the *San Francisco Examiner*. *Dune*, his first book in the Dune series, won both Hugo and Nebula awards. He has also written *Destination: Void*; *The Godmakers*; and *The Dosadi Experiment*. He died in 1986.

God Emperor of Dune   PUTNAM, 1981
Science Fiction. Originally a dry planet inhabited by giant sandworms and the Fremen who recycle water, Dune has become transformed into a more normal and wetter world. It is 3,500 years after the events of the original trilogy. There is one small area of desert left, and this belongs to Leto II, once human and now almost totally transformed into a sandworm. He is the God Emperor, and the last living sandworm, and he must survive for the Fremen, who worship him and the mind-expanding melange that he produces.

Heretics of Dune   PUTNAM, 1984
Science Fiction. Intrigue and a deadly conflict for power take place on the planet Gammu in this fifth volume of the Dune cycle. The Bene Gesserit Sisterhood is protecting their ghola project in the person of the reincarnated Duncan Idaho, although some of the sisterhood seek Duncan's death. Meanwhile, the Tleilaxu are plotting revenge, Leto II may be returning, and a young girl is found who has power over the worms.

HERSEY, JOHN

Born in Tientsin, China, 1914; he moved to the United States with his family in 1925. He graduated from Yale and spent one summer as secretary to Sinclair Lewis. He also worked for *Time* and *Life* magazines as a journalist and war correspondent from 1942 to 1946. His first novel, *A Bell for Adano*, won a Pulitzer Prize and was followed by such novels as *The Wall*; *Hiroshima*; *The War Lover*; and *Too Far to Walk*. Hersey has also recently published the autobiographical book *Blues*.

Under the Eye of the Storm   KNOPF, 1967
Drama. Tom Medlar, along with his wife and another couple, sails his boat *Harmony* off the New England coast and into a hurricane. Tom's isolation from the others grows with the storm as he dedicates himself to all the sailing details and does not realize that everything around him may not be as he sees it.

HIGGINS, JACK. SEE PATTERSON, HARRY.

HILL, RUTH BEEBE
Born in Ohio, 1913; educated at Western Reserve University. She is a journalist whose interest in American Indians led to 25 years of work on *Hanta Yo*. She traveled throughout the United States and Canada, talked to many Indians, learned dialects, and did other research.

Hanta Yo   DOUBLEDAY, 1979
Saga–Historical Novel. This is a fictionalized account of a record kept by a member of the Sioux from 1794 to 1835. It shows their seasonal movements across the plains, their ceremonies, battles, and ways of thinking. It is also a story of friendship between two boys, Ahbleza, the son of a warrior-leader, and Tonweya, the son of a hunter. To keep it as accurate as possible to the Indian idiom, the author translated the original manuscript into Dakotah, and then back into English.

HOFFMAN, E. T. A., WITH ILLUSTRATOR MAURICE SENDAK
Hoffman was a 19th-century German writer whose tale *The Nutcracker and the Mouse King* has become a children's Christmas classic, best known from the Tchaikovsky ballet. Sendak, a modern illustrator of best-selling children's books, returned to the original Hoffman tale for the Pacific Northwest Ballet production and the subsequent book. It is a much more complicated tale, Sendak observes in the introduction, than the Tchaikovsky version suggests, and more concerned with nightmares than sugarplums.

Nutcracker   CROWN, 1984
Juvenile. Christmas toys come alive for a little girl, including her toy soldier, Nutcracker, who has been scorned and damaged by her brother Fritz. What follows is a series of adventures in the kingdom of the dolls, with a fierce battle between Nutcracker and the evil Mouse King, a story of a doll princess, and the history of the hard nut. The little girl, Marie, is increasingly drawn into these adventures, travels with her toy soldier and knight into fairyland, and becomes a princess herself. Translated from the German by Ralph Manheim.

HOLT, VICTORIA (PSEUDONYM OF ELEANOR BURFORD HIBBERT)
Born in London, 1906. She read widely from a very early age, and attended secondary school until she had to stop for lack of money. After writing short stories that were immediately successful, she experimented with writing a novel that would appeal to many people. She wrote historical novels under the name of Jean Plaidy and then turned to romantic suspense under the name Victoria Holt. *Mistress of Mellyn* was her first best seller, achieving worldwide success. She has written over 150 novels under seven different pseudonyms for an average of three books a year. Recent novels are *The Road to Paradise Island* and *Secret for a Nightingale* (1986).

The Legend of the Seventh Virgin   DOUBLEDAY, 1965
   Drama. Kerensa Carlee, a servant girl, aspires to be mistress of Abbas.
   Proud, resolute, and determined, she has been taught well by her
   Granny Bee to let nothing stand in the way of what she wants. She
   betrays a friend who gave her kindness and help. But then Kerensa
   herself is betrayed.

Menfreya in the Morning   DOUBLEDAY, 1966
   Suspense. Harriet Delvaney longs for the excitement of the Menfrey
   family. But when she finally becomes a Menfrey herself, her happiness
   is replaced by suspicion, treachery, and a secret family legend.

The King of the Castle   DOUBLEDAY, 1967
   Suspense. Dallas Lawson sets out from England to take her late father's
   place as a restorer of art treasures in a French chateau. As she wins the
   trust of the household, she soon discovers a count who may have killed
   his wife, a disturbed young girl, and a lost fortune in jewels.

The Queen's Confession   DOUBLEDAY, 1968
   Historical Novel. Fictionalized history of Marie Antoinette as told
   through her memoirs. She tells how she was sent from home at 14 for
   an arranged marriage with the French dauphin, and how she disre-
   garded etiquette and was impulsive and extravagant. But she shows,
   too, the intrigue at court, the hostility to a queen that was not French,
   and the growing signs of revolution. When violence finally engulfs her
   and her family, she faces her fate with courage.
      The novel recreates the details of court life, the sudden shifts of
   public opinion, and the spirit of the time. A bibliography is provided.

The Shivering Sands   DOUBLEDAY, 1969
   Mystery. A young woman attempts to trace her lost sister who has disappeared at an estate near the quicksands of Kent. There she takes a
   job as a piano teacher, and soon finds herself caught in a mystery involving her three young charges, a bitter young man accused of killing
   his brother, and another disappearance.

The Secret Woman   DOUBLEDAY, 1970
   Suspense. Young Anna Brett is raised by her aunt to be a dealer of
   antiques. She develops a close friendship with the girl who becomes her
   aunt's nurse, and is intrigued by a sea captain who belongs to the Castle
   Crediton. Upon the aunt's death, the nurse takes a position at the castle
   and soon leads Anna into a more exciting future, but one of deception
   and death.

The Shadow of the Lynx   DOUBLEDAY, 1971
   Drama. After Lynx has been falsely convicted of a crime and sent to
   Australia, he vows to make the estate of Whiteladies his. His young ward
   Nora and his son are drawn into his web of influence in this story of
   romance and revenge.

On the Night of the Seventh Moon   DOUBLEDAY, 1972
   Mystery. While attending school in Germany, Helena Trant becomes
   lost in the woods and is found by a handsome, mysterious man. Al-

though she knows him for only a few hours, she becomes obsessed with meeting him again. But when she finally does, she suddenly finds herself surrounded by confusion and treachery.

The House of a Thousand Lanterns   DOUBLEDAY, 1974
Suspense. Jane Lindsay grows up in the home of a collector of Chinese art, and soon she, too, learns about the Oriental treasures. When she finds herself living in Hong Kong, the charm and allure of the Orient mask the treachery of those around her, and she almost falls victim to superstitions. In a land where women have few rights and little power, she must take command of her life and a profitable business, and make a decision about marriage.

The Pride of the Peacock   DOUBLEDAY, 1976
Drama. A dying man's wish finds (Opal) Jessica Clavering married to his adopted son, but not out of love. Soon Jessica is whisked away with her new husband to Australia, where they are co-owners of a vast opal mine. Here they must come to terms with the superstition surrounding the opal called the Green Flash, and also learn their true feelings for each other.

HOWATCH, SUSAN

Born in England, 1940. Howatch earned a law degree from King's College, London, and returned to England after spending some years in New York City. Her novels include *The Wheel of Fortune*; *The Shrouded Walls*; and *Glittering Images* (1987).

Penmarric   SIMON & SCHUSTER, 1971
Saga–Historical Novel. The great stone house of Penmarric, on the rugged Cornwall cliffs, is the center of conflicts engaging the Castallack family. Here Mark sires his legitimate and illegitimate children; and here the children grow up, torn between rival families and their own ideas of love, justice, and truth.

Cashelmara   SIMON & SCHUSTER, 1974
Saga–Historical Novel. The estate of Cashelmara in Ireland is home to three generations of a British aristocratic family. The effeminate son Patrick whittles away his inheritance with an unscrupulous friend, while Patrick's wife brings new conflicts to the Irish estate already buffeted by famine, mismanagement, and feuds. People die mysteriously, and it is left to Patrick's son Ned to decide what avenging needs to be done.

The Rich Are Different   SIMON & SCHUSTER, 1977
Saga. The novel follows five people in the world of investment banking from the Roaring Twenties through the stock market crash to the coming of war in 1940. Love and betrayal are mixed in the lives of banker Paul Van Zale, his wife, his British mistress, a partner, and a protégé.

Sins of the Father   SIMON & SCHUSTER, 1980
Saga. In this sequel to *The Rich Are Different*, two protégés of Paul Van Zale continue their battle for power in the world of Wall Street banking.

Their struggle affects others as the sins of the fathers are passed on to the children.

HUMPHREY, WILLIAM

Born in Texas, 1924, where most of his novels are set; he attended Southern Methodist University and the University of Texas. He has written *Home from the Hill* (1958) and *Proud Flesh* (1973), as well as short stories.

The Ordways   KNOPF, 1965

Saga. A tale of a very unusual family spanning 100 years and the entire state of Texas. We cross it twice—one time in a 62-person, 14-car cavalcade. The family history, recalled on Graveyard Working Day, includes a disreputable Civil War ancestor, the magnificent odyssey of Grandfather Ed, and the mysterious Mr. Vinson, who would like to be an Ordway too.

IRVING, JOHN (WINSLOW)

Born in New Hampshire, 1942; educated at the University of Pittsburgh, the University of Vienna, and the University of New Hampshire. He was a professor of English at Mount Holyoke College and a Fellow of the National Endowment for the Arts. Other novels include *Setting Free the Bears* (1968), *The Water-Method Man* (1972), and *The 158-Pound Marriage* (1972).

The World According to Garp   DUTTON, 1978

Drama. The novel tells the story of Garp's life from his begetting, to the bizarre way he got his name, through his grim childhood, to his career as an immensely talented novelist. The end of his story is as strange and violent as the beginning.

The Hotel New Hampshire   DUTTON, 1981

Drama. Twenty-five years in the life of the strange Berry family from Dairy, New Hampshire, as narrated by the middle son of the family. He describes their lives as they grow older in three hotels, all called the Hotel New Hampshire, and live with a bear and a dog named Sorrow. Tragedy afflicts them through death, rape, and blindness as they try to pursue their dreams.

ISAACS, SUSAN

Born in Brooklyn, 1943; educated at Queen's College. Isaacs is the author of the book and the screenplay *Compromising Positions*, and the screenplay *Hello Again*.

Almost Paradise   HARPER & ROW, 1984

Drama. The story of Nicholas and Jane Cobleigh, their childhood, parents, marriage, careers, and conflicts. It is given dramatic focus by the Prologue's warning of a tragedy.

JACKSON, CHARLES REGINALD

Born in New Jersey, 1903. As a young man he was ill with tuberculosis and went to Switzerland for his health. He started writing then, and went on to write for radio, television, and movies. He has published a number of short stories, some of which are collected in *The Sunnier Side*. His first published novel was *The Lost Weekend* (1944), which as a movie won Academy Awards for Best Picture and Best Script. Other novels include *The Fall of Valor* and *The Outer Edges*. He died in 1968.

A Second-Hand Life   MACMILLAN, 1967

Sex—Drama. The lives of two friends from a small town in upstate New York are depicted. Winnie is a nymphomaniac, and Harry is incapable of intimacy with anyone. Each has had one brief romance, but together they have had a 30-year friendship as they lead their second-hand lives.

JAFFE, RONA

Born in New York City, 1932; educated at the Dalton School and Radcliffe. She became an editor at Fawcett at age 20 and published her first book, *The Best of Everything*, at age 26. Other novels include *The Other Woman*; *Mazes and Monsters*; and a sequel to *Class Reunion*, *After the Reunion*.

Class Reunion   DELACORTE, 1979

Sex—Drama. The narrative follows the lives of four women from their Radcliffe graduation to their 20th reunion in the 1970s. The emphasis is on their romantic relationships and the various marriages, divorces, and new alliances that they make.

JAKES, JOHN

Born in Illinois, 1932; educated at De Pauw and Ohio State University. Before achieving fame as a best-selling author, he wrote some 40 novels in a variety of genres (science fiction, mystery, children's books), as well as nonfiction, short stories, and plays. He is the author of the four books known as the Kent Family Chronicles, and the conclusion to the *North and South* trilogy, *Heaven and Hell* (1987).

North and South   HARCOURT, 1982

Historical Novel—War. The story of two families in pre—Civil War America and of romance, treachery, honor, and death. The base of the story is formed by the bond of friendship between George Hazard from the North and Orry Main from the South, who meet at West Point as cadets. Jakes uses historical facts and sentiments to give his characters life.

Love and War   HARCOURT, 1984

Historical Novel—War. The book continues where *North and South* ends. With the onset of the Civil War, the friendship of George and Orry is tested when they find themselves generals on different sides. Plots that began in the previous book come to some conclusions in this story.

JAMES, P. D. (PHYLLIS DOROTHY)

Born in England, 1920. Without the financial means to attend college, she began work in the civil service and progressed through the ranks while going to night school and caring for her children and invalid husband. She has worked in police courts and served as a magistrate in London. In a Book-of-the-Month Club interview, James says that her books deal with "the contrivances by which human beings manage to survive psychologically in this world." She has published mysteries and tales of psychological suspense, including *An Unsuitable Job for a Woman* and *The Black Tower. A Taste for Death* was published in 1986.

Innocent Blood SCRIBNER, 1980

Drama. Adopted Philippa Palfrey sets out at age 18 to discover who her real parents are, and gets more than she bargained for. A tale of crimes, past and present, and how people go beyond the bounds of conventional morality to cope with the need for love.

JENKINS, DAN

Born in Texas, 1929. He has worked as a sports editor and reporter, and is currently a senior writer at *Sports Illustrated*. The author of several books, he lives in Manhattan with his wife.

Semi-Tough ATHENEUM, 1972

Drama–Sex. Billy Clyde Puckett, halfback for the New York Giants, is in Los Angeles to play in the Superbowl and to write a book about the events surrounding the big game. Most of the novel is concerned with the week before the game, during which Billy Clyde introduces us to his off-the-wall friends, and talks about sex, restaurants, minorities, and the hated Jets.

JONES, JAMES

Born in Illinois, 1921. He joined the army at the age of 18 and served in the Pacific from 1939 to 1944. These war experiences became the basis for his trilogy *From Here to Eternity* (1951), *The Thin Red Line* (1962), and *Whistle* (1978). In addition to his novels he has also written short stories. He died in 1977.

Go to the Widow-Maker DELACORTE, 1967

Sex–Drama. Famous playwright Ron Grant must find out what it means to be masculine. So he goes diving, tests his courage killing sharks, and tries to break off an affair and begin a marriage. As the characters interact with each other, they offer Grant their own definitions of manhood: his aging mistress, his wife, his drinking buddy, who is the husband of his mistress, and a six-foot-two, well-larded diving instructor. All want a relationship with him.

Whistle DELACORTE, 1978

War. Four men from the same infantry company are sent home to a hospital in the States. They are so marked by war, however, and their bonds to each other, that they cannot adjust to any other life. We see the wounded hero, the tough sergeant who looks out for his men, and the soldier whose fights keep him one step from court-martial. Yet they are really the same character, plagued by the same nightmares, and suffering the same fate.

Thirty years in the writing, the book was almost completed at Jones's death. The last few chapters were sketched in by editor Willie Morris from the author's notes.

JONG, ERICA

Born in New York City, 1942; educated at Barnard and Columbia University. She achieved popularity with her first novel, *Fear of Flying* (1973), and has also published collections of poems. A novel, *Serenissima*, appeared in 1987.

How to Save Your Own Life   HOLT, RINEHART & WINSTON, 1977
Sex–Drama. Isadora Wing realizes she must end her marriage if she is to save her life. As she sets out to do so, she gives an account of her feelings, friends, and past experiences.

Fanny   NEW AMERICAN LIBRARY, 1980
Historical Novel–Sex. A feminist reinterpretation of the adventures of Fanny Hill, first told by John Cleland in his 18th-century novel. In Jong's account, Fanny overcomes adversity by her own power and courage. Seduced at 17 by her foster father, she leaves home; she joins a coven of witches and then a band of highwaymen. She works in a house of ill repute to save money for her lover and unborn child, and has many other adventures along the way. The 20th-century storyteller successfully maintains the 18th-century literary style.

KAUFMAN, BEL

Born in Berlin, Germany; educated at Hunter College and Columbia University, with highest honors. Denied a license to teach, she was living in poverty until the publication of *Up the Down Staircase*. She has since worked as a professor of English, has lectured throughout the country, and has made many television and radio appearances. She has also written short stories, articles, and lyrics for musicals. Her book *Love, etc.* was published in 1979.

Up the Down Staircase   PRENTICE-HALL, 1964
Drama. The story of a teacher's first year in a New York City high school. The story is told through a series of letters, administration memos, and student compositions, as Sylvia Barrett tries to keep her ideals and decide what kind of teaching she wants to do.

An anniversary edition of the book was published in 1989, with a new preface by the author.

KAYE, M. M. (MARY MARGARET)

Born in India, 1909. She was educated in England and returned to India, marrying a British officer and raising a family there. She has also lived in Kenya, Northern Ireland, Egypt, and Germany, and has written children's books under the name of Mollie Kaye. She worked on *The Far Pavilions* for 15 years.

The Far Pavilions   ST. MARTINS, 1978

Historical Novel. A story of 19th-century India told from the point of view of Ash, a British military officer raised as a Hindu. Sympathetic to both cultures, he is never fully accepted by either; and while he goes on secret missions for England, he cannot convince his superiors of the urgent information he reports. Ash falls in love with Juli, an Indian princess who also confronts a choice between two cultures. Their love story is set against a background of events—of famine, invasion, and racial conflict—in India during a time of change.

The book is 955 pages in length, with a glossary of Indian terms.

Shadow of the Moon   ST. MARTINS, 1979

Historical Novel. Again Kaye writes of life in 19th-century India. A young British woman comes to India in an arranged marriage and falls in love with a British military officer who is her husband's assistant. They experience at first hand, with their own lives at stake, the Indian Mutiny of 1857.

This is an expanded version of a novel first published in 1956. It includes a glossary of Indian terms.

KAZAN, ELIA

Born in Constantinople, 1909; educated at Williams College and Yale Drama School. He became known as a director in theatre and film, winning two Oscars, including one for *On the Waterfront*, and three Tonys, including one for *Death of a Salesman*. He has also written the novel *The Understudy* and the autobiography *Elia Kazan: A Life*.

The Arrangement   STEIN & DAY, 1967

Drama. After an attempt at suicide and a mental breakdown, a man begins to strip away the lies and compromises of his life. He has had two jobs, two women in his life, and even two names. Now he must find out how he really wants to live.

The Assassins   STEIN & DAY, 1972

Drama—War. There are murders at the beginning and the end of the book, but the biggest crimes occur in the middle, as a community tries to protect an air force sergeant who has killed a radical youth. Kazan is sympathetic to the youth culture of the time and critical of a society that trains men to kill and rewards them for doing so.

KEMELMAN, HARRY

Born in Boston, 1908; educated at Boston University and Harvard. He taught briefly in the Boston public schools, and in 1965 was the recipient of the Edgar Award for the best first novel, with *Friday the Rabbi Slept Late*. Other books include *Tuesday the Rabbi Saw Red*; *Wednesday the Rabbi*

Got Wet; *Thursday the Rabbi Walked Out*; and *One Fine Day the Rabbi Bought a Cross* (1986).

Saturday the Rabbi Went Hungry   CROWN, 1966

Mystery–Religion. Conservative David Small is a young rabbi in a small town. When a nonpracticing Jew is found dead, apparently a suicide, the rabbi takes it upon himself to secure a proper burial. But most of the Jewish community is upset by this; so the rabbi investigates the death further using the logic of his religious teachings.

Sunday the Rabbi Stayed Home   PUTNAM, 1969

Mystery–Religion. A social study of the problems of the 1960s. Rabbi Small comes to the aid of youths involved with marijuana and murder. Once again he uses the logic of his religion to solve a crime. The author also shows the trivial conflicts and politics that take place in the rabbi's congregation.

KEYES, FRANCIS PARKINSON

Born in Virginia, 1885; educated at George Washington University and Bates. She began writing fiction in 1919. Among nearly 50 novels, she wrote the famous *Dinner at Antoine's* (1948) and *Madame Castel's Lodger* (1962), as well as *The Heritage* (1968) and *All Flags Flying* (1972). She died in 1970.

The Explorer   MCGRAW, 1964

Drama. Unusual conditions for marriage are established between famous explorer Nicolas Hale and Margaret, a Virginia estate owner. In spite of themselves they fall in love, but their relationship is tested as Nicolas tries to discover his dream of a lost city in Peru.

I, the King   MCGRAW, 1966

Historical Novel. The story of King Philip of Spain in the 17th century and the women who shared his life: Queen Isabel, beautiful and intelligent, a partner with him in fun and government; Inés, the actress who loved him and gave him a son; and María de Ágreda, an abbess who offered spiritual support in his aging years. During Philip's reign, Spain lost her position as a great power. The novel shows the bad advice he received and the problem of producing an heir to the throne. Authentic letters from the time are included.

KING, STEPHEN (ALSO USED THE PSEUDONYM RICHARD BACHMAN)

Born in Portland, Maine, 1947; educated at the University of Maine, where he began publishing stories. His first published novel was *Carrie*, followed by *Salem's Lot*. King has also written screenplays, including *Creepshow*; *Cat's Eye*; *Maximum Overdrive*; and *Silver Bullet*. Recent novels include *It*; *The Eyes of the Dragon*; *Misery*; and *The Tommyknockers*. He lives in Maine with his wife, Tabitha, and their three children.

The Shining   DOUBLEDAY, 1977

Horror. When little Danny Torrance and his parents move into an empty, isolated hotel in Colorado, they do not find the peace and quiet that they expected. The boy has visions of horrors in the hotel through an extra sense that an old black man calls "the Shining." But Danny finds even more terror when he sees what the hotel has done to his father.

The Dead Zone   VIKING, 1979

Science Fiction–Suspense. John Smith awakes from a four-year coma with the terrible power to see the future of the people he touches. To what extent can he change the future, and does he want to? What are the costs to him—and the world—if he does or does not try?

Firestarter   VIKING, 1980

Science Fiction–Suspense. Victims of a psychology experiment, eight-year-old Charlie McGee and her father are on the run from a government group called the Shop. The father can put suggestions into people's minds, and the little girl can start fires with her mind. When the Shop does catch and confine them, things start getting hot.

Cujo   VIKING, 1981

Horror. King gives us a realistic monster in a family pet who chases a rabbit and gets rabies. Cujo knows that something is wrong with him because he has the "baddog" feeling, but he does not know what to do. As the disease progresses, he holds four-year-old Tad and his mother at bay in their disabled car, and touches other people's lives, too, before his reign of terror is ended.

King admitted in an interview (Underwood, p. 51) that he did not plan the ending for the story but "discovered" as he was writing that it happened that way.

Different Seasons   VIKING, 1982

Short Stories–Horror–Science Fiction. This is a collection of four stories, one for each season of the year. King gives us an inside look at human nature with a variety of characters. Prison inmates are seen in a humorous light; a youth is influenced by Nazi ideals; several young boys anticipate seeing a dead body; and we are shown inside a unique club for gentlemen.

Pet Sematary   DOUBLEDAY, 1983

Horror. When Louis Creed moved his family into a new home, he never expected that a pet cemetery went with the neighborhood. An elderly man takes the Creeds down the "safe path" to the cemetery, and it seems to be a pleasant enough place. But after the family experiences death, Louis learns of the immense terror lurking there.

Christine   VIKING, 1983

Horror. Arnie Cunningham, plagued by an awkward adolescence, has only one friend, a popular boy named Dennis. But when Arnie buys a '58 Plymouth Fury, things start changing for him. He starts to fix it up, and soon he, too, is looking better. Christine is not a normal car, however; and all the people who were mean to Arnie are going to be sorry.

Thinner   NEW AMERICAN LIBRARY, 1984
Horror. Billy Halleck has a nice family and a job in New York City. Then Billy accidentally kills an old Gypsy woman, and his life takes a chilling turn for the worse. He begins losing weight at a terrifying pace, and so begins his desperate hunt for the curse that has been placed upon him. The search takes him far from his familiar surroundings and builds to a macabre conclusion.

King wrote this book under the name Richard Bachman.

The Talisman   PUTNAM, 1984
Science Fiction–Horror. In a tourist town during the off-season, young Jack befriends an old man who already seems to know him. Jack's mother is dying of cancer, and the man tells the boy that he, Jack, must travel into a parallel world in order to save her and her counterpart in the other world. His mission is to retrieve a talisman, but it is a long and dangerous journey where evil men and creatures try to stop him, and a werewolf befriends him.

Coauthored with Peter Straub.

KNEBEL, FLETCHER (PRONOUNCED KUH-NABUL)
Born in Dayton, Ohio, 1911; educated at Miami University in Ohio. He served as a lieutenant in the navy from 1942 to 1945. Knebel worked from 1937 to 1964 as Washington correspondent for the *Cleveland Plain Dealer* and Cowles Publications. He wrote a humorous column for 15 years called "Potomac Fever," and was president of the Washington reporters' Gridiron Club. He collaborated with Charles Bailey on two best-selling novels, *Seven Days in May* and *Convention*, and has published another thriller, *Sabotage* (1986).

Night of Camp David   HARPER & ROW, 1965
American Politics–Suspense. Handsome, easygoing Jim MacVeagh is in line to be vice-president until he realizes that something is very wrong at the White House—and it could lead to nuclear war. Knebel draws on his years as Washington correspondent for background details of life in the nation's capital.

Vanished   DOUBLEDAY, 1968
American Politics–Suspense. Why has a close friend of the president disappeared without a trace? And why has a prominent scientist disappeared also? What stakes are involved for a senator and a CIA chief, and why will the president not tell what he knows? These are some of the questions facing a presidential press secretary, while reporters sniff a scandal, and public support for the president falls.

Dark Horse   DOUBLEDAY, 1972
American Politics. Honest, ordinary Eddie Quinn, car-lover and New Jersey turnpike commissioner, suddenly finds himself nominated for president, and he might even win! Eddie holds to his ideals through a

series of exciting adventures all the way to election night. The story is a political fantasy, but an entertaining one.

KOTZWINKLE, WILLIAM

Born in Pennsylvania, 1938; educated at Rider College and Penn State. He won the O. Henry Prize in 1975, and the World Fantasy Award at the Third World Fantasy Convention in 1977. Kotzwinkle is the author of numerous books and stories, including *Doctor Rat*; *Fata Morgana*; *Nightbook*; and *The Exile* (1987).

E.T.: The Extraterrestrial   MCA, 1982

Science Fiction. While collecting plant specimens, a strange being is accidentally left behind on Earth. He forms a special bond with a little boy named Elliot, but must return to his own kind in order to live. Meanwhile, government officials are attempting to capture E.T., and it is up to Elliot and his friends to save him.

Based on the screenplay by Melissa Mathison.

KRANTZ, JUDITH

Born in New York City, 1927; educated at Wellesley. She worked as a fashion editor and contributing writer to *McCall's* and *Ladies' Home Journal*. After 27 years as a journalist, she began her first novel, *Scruples*, in 1976. She has also written *I'll Take Manhattan*.

Scruples   CROWN, 1978

Glamour–Sex. Billy Orsini, rich and beautiful, makes her Hollywood boutique into a "raging tearing success." In the second half of the book, she marries a film producer and joins him in making a movie. The action follows Billy and the other characters from Hollywood to Cannes to the Academy Award nominations, and gives us the names of all the restaurants, designers, and resorts along the way.

Princess Daisy   CROWN, 1980

Glamour–Sex. A modern fairy tale, complete with a beautiful spirited princess, an evil relative, and a dark secret to be guarded from the day of her birth. Daisy is born to wealth and fame, the daughter of a Russian nobleman and an American actress. But she is beset by tragedies and betrayals, and must make her own way back to fame and fortune.

Mistral's Daughter   CROWN, 1982

Saga–Glamour–Sex. Three generations of beautiful women are involved with the artist Mistral. Maggie is his model and his love, while her daughter Teddy is the mother of his child, Fauve. All of the women are illegitimate children and have successful careers as models. Short histories of all the characters are provided.

L'AMOUR, LOUIS DEARBORN

Born in North Dakota, 1908; self-educated. He received an honorary degree from Jamestown College and lectured at numerous universities. With more than 200 million copies of his books still in print, he is regarded as the top American best-selling author. L'Amour was awarded a Congressional Medal of Honor for Literature and a Presidential Medal of Freedom. He wrote 101 books, including *Hondo*; *Son of a Wanted Man*; *The Cherokee Trail*; and *Jubal Sackett*. He died in 1988 while completing his autobiography, *Education of a Wandering Man*.

The Lonesome Gods BANTAM, 1983

Western–Historical Novel. In the 1840s, a young boy goes west with his dying father to southern California. He grows up with Indians in the desert and mountains, and with a businesswoman in Los Angeles. But young Johannes discovers that he has many enemies who want him dead, so he must learn quickly how to survive.

The Walking Drum BANTAM, 1984

Historical Novel–Adventure. In the 12th century a young man, Kerbouchard, leaves his home in Brittany in search of his corsair father. He takes on different roles in his travels, as prisoner, seaman, merchant, and physician, but always he is a scholar and a warrior. His path leads through Europe to Arab lands and the Russian steppes, and along the way he makes as many enemies as he does friends.

LE CARRE, JOHN (PSEUDONYM OF DAVID CORNWELL)

Born in England, 1931; educated at Berne and Oxford. He taught at Eton, and was in the British foreign service when he began writing. Unable to use his real name because of government restrictions, he adopted the name le Carre. His first novel was *Call for the Dead* (1961), followed by *A Murder of Quality*. He has recently published *A Perfect Spy*.

The Spy Who Came in from the Cold COWARD, MCCANN, 1964

Spy. Alec Leamas of British intelligence must complete one last perilous assignment before he can retire. He will fake a defection to East Berlin, thereby working for his country undercover. But the horrible suspicion begins to grow that he is to be abandoned there. It looks like the double agent is being double-crossed.

Graham Greene called this "The best spy novel I have ever read."

The Looking Glass War COWARD, MCCANN, 1965

Spy. Petty rivalries and dreams of past glory plague a department of British security. One after another, three men are sent to East Germany seeking evidence of a secret missile base. But there is no support for each man as he makes his run. After the failure of the first two, a third man, who was in the war, is given a crash training course. If he fails, he will be on his own.

A Small Town in Germany COWARD, MCCANN, 1968

Spy. A British official defects from the Bonn embassy with top-secret papers. He was, however, only a temporary worker with no security clearance. How did this happen, and why did he do it? Investigator Alan Turner goes to the small town in Germany, where bureaucratic and personal dealings hold the answers, if he can only ask the right questions of the right people.

Tinker, Tailor, Soldier, Spy KNOPF, 1974

Spy. A major personnel change in the Circus has had George Smiley replaced, but now they need him. There is a double agent from Moscow who is undermining British intelligence. So Smiley must retrace his way through 20 years of Circus history to find which of his friends or fellow workers is the traitor.

The Honourable Schoolboy KNOPF, 1977

Spy. Jerry Westerby, "the Honourable Schoolboy," is a seasoned agent recruited by George Smiley: his job, to find out why Russian money is being paid into the account of a Hong Kong businessman. The trail leads from London to Southeast Asia and shows, through le Carré's carefully researched account, the costs of war to the survivors.

Smiley's People KNOPF, 1980

Spy. George Smiley, once chief of Secret Service, comes out of retirement to discover what an old friend and fellow worker was trying to tell him when he was killed. Soon he finds himself caught in a final confrontation with Karla, his mortal enemy and opposite in the Soviet Union. This is Smiley's story all the way, and he is still the best at his craft.

The Little Drummer Girl KNOPF, 1983

Spy. Charlie, a young actress romantically drawn to various political causes, is recruited by the Israelis to capture a Palestinian terrorist. Le Carré conveys the atmosphere of Middle Eastern intrigue as the plot works through to the final deception.

LEONARD, ELMORE

Born in New Orleans, 1925; educated at the University of Detroit. He wrote westerns and crime fiction part-time, and advertising copy for a living. Now he writes television pilots and films in addition to his novels. Two recent books are *Bandits* and *Touch*. "I'm not a good narrative writer," he admits. "I put all my energies into my characters, and let my characters carry it" (*Never in Doubt*, p. 91).

Glitz ARBOR HOUSE, 1985

Suspense–Sex. A Miami policeman goes to San Juan to recuperate from a bullet wound, and to see a girlfriend who is a hooker. There he runs into a psychopath he once sent to prison, and who now wants revenge on the detective. The two men stalk each other to a final confrontation.

LEVIN, IRA

Born in New York City, 1929; educated at New York University. He served in the Army Signal Corps. He has written short stories, lyrics, film scripts, and plays, including *No Time for Sergeants* (1955). Other novels are *A Kiss before Dying*; *This Perfect Day*; and *The Stepford Wives*.

Rosemary's Baby RANDOM HOUSE, 1967

Horror. Rosemary and Guy Woodhouse move into a Manhattan apartment house with a history of witchcraft and violent death. After they meet their elderly upstairs neighbors, Rosemary finds herself caught in a tightening web of supernatural terror from which there may be no escape.

The Boys from Brazil   RANDOM HOUSE, 1976
International Intrigue. Ninety-four men are scheduled to be killed, each a civil servant near retirement, each living quietly and unknown to the others. Why? Elderly Yakov Lieberman, head of the War Crimes Information Center, sets out to find the answer. He must face and defeat his mortal enemy and then make one final terrifying decision.

LOFTS, NORAH

Born in England, 1904. A prolific writer (she called herself "a compulsive writer"), she published many novels of history and the supernatural, such as *A Rose for Virtue*; *The Old Priory*; and *The Haunting of Gad's Hall*. She also wrote under the pen name of Peter Curtis. Lofts lived in an ancient house in England which provided great atmosphere for her work. She died in 1983.

The Lost Queen   DOUBLEDAY, 1969
Historical Novel. Set in England and Denmark in the 1700s. Lofts tells the story of a little-known historical figure—Caroline, sister to the English King George III, who marries Christian, King of Denmark. Christian, short in stature and retarded from birth, is going insane from syphilis. He has mind enough left, however, to make brutal and arbitrary decrees in his court and to try to make Caroline's life miserable. Her own family does little to help: the British king is weak himself and has problems with his American colonies.

LORD, BETTE BAO

Born in Shanghai, 1938; she came to the United States in 1946 when her father, an official with the Chinese government, was assigned to this country. She graduated from Tufts University and received a master's degree from the Fletcher School of Law and Diplomacy. She now lives in the United States with her husband, who has served as president of the Council on Foreign Relations. A visit to China and reunion with her relatives inspired the writing of *Spring Moon*.

Spring Moon   HARPER & ROW, 1981
Historical Novel. A story of China from 1892 to the 1970s, capturing the spirit and details of life before and after the Revolution. At the center of the story is Spring Moon, a young girl when the novel begins and an elderly matriarch at the end, when five generations of the family gather for a reunion at the site of the family graves. Through a time of great social upheaval, tradition and continuities remain.

LUDLUM, ROBERT

Born in New York City, 1927; educated at Wesleyan. He served in the Marines in World War II. Ludlum worked as an actor and producer on Broadway and in television, with credits in more than 200 television shows. He then totally left the theatre and began writing, producing a top best seller every year or every other year. Recent novels are *The Bourne Supremacy* and *The Icarus Agenda*. Ludlum fans should watch for the books by Jonathan Ryder, too.

The Matlock Paper   DOUBLEDAY, 1973
Suspense. A giant conspiracy is infiltrating American universities, and James Matlock, professor and Vietnam veteran, has been selected to stop it. But Matlock has not been told what he is really being asked to do—or that he is not expected to come out alive. He cannot rely on his own colleagues for help because they, too, may be part of the conspiracy.

The Rhinemann Exchange   DIAL, 1974
Spy. In the autumn of 1943 the outcome of the war is still in doubt, with Germany and the U.S. each needing material possessed by the other. A handful of military industrialists in both nations attempt to engineer a trade so that the war can be fought to its conclusion. American agent David Spaulding risks his life to make the exchange without knowing its deadly purpose.

The Gemini Contenders   DOUBLEDAY, 1976
International Intrigue. As the Germans move closer in World War II, some monks bury a vault in the Italian Alps. Its contents, if known, would tear apart the Christian world. The book is divided into two parts: in Book I a wealthy young Italian playboy must keep the secret of the vault, and in Book II his sons inherit the problem.

The Chancellor Manuscript   DIAL PRESS, 1977
Suspense. J. Edgar Hoover is murdered to obtain files threatening the lives of many Americans, although half of the files are found to be missing. Writer Peter Chancellor is used as decoy by a secret group to recover the lost information. But as members of the group begin to be murdered, Peter comes to realize that the files may be sought for very different purposes—one, to protect innocent people, and another, to cover up a massacre that occurred more than 20 years before.

The Holcroft Covenant   RICHARD MAREK, 1978
International Intrigue. Three heirs must be found to sign a document providing $780 million stolen from the Nazis in World War II, to be used to aid the survivors and descendants of the Holocaust. But one of the heirs, American architect Noel Holcroft, does not know that the funds will really be used to lay the foundations for the Fourth Reich. As Noel fights for his life, he must uncover what the document means and try to stop the plan from being carried out.

The Matarese Circle   RICHARD MAREK, 1979
Spy. A small circle of men called the Matarese can take over the world in two years' time. Its members include the highest officials of the major governments. This global conspiracy can be stopped only if two individuals—an American and a Russian secret agent—will work together. But they have already sworn to kill each other.

The Bourne Identity
RICHARD MAREK, 1980

Spy. A man has been found at sea, shot and left for dead. He has also been subjected to plastic surgery and does not remember who he is. Slowly, as his skills and talents come back, he knows he can fight for his life, steal, hide, and outwit opponents. Then other memories follow, at first erratic and unreliable. Is he the assassin Cain, used as a lure to catch an even greater assassin? And why is the government in Washington trying to kill him?

The Parsifal Mosaic
RANDOM HOUSE, 1982

Spy. Michael Havelock, son of a Czech partisan, is a U.S. undercover agent and a protégé of the secretary of state. When his girlfriend and coworker is murdered by his agency, Michael is driven nearly insane. Was she really a double agent? And is she really dead? He sets out wildly and alone to try to answer these questions and finds a conspiracy, planned for decades, that threatens the end of civilization.

The Aquitaine Progression
RANDOM HOUSE, 1984

International Intrigue. A conspiratorial group is staging violence in key European capitals so that it can move in with its own military government. Joel Converse, an American lawyer in Geneva and ex-POW, must help end the conspiracy. Hunted by Aquitaine and tormented by his own past memories, Converse must be willing to call on his old fighting skills in a race against time.

LURIE, ALISON

Born in Chicago, 1926; educated at Radcliffe. She taught in the English Department at Cornell. Her novels include *Imaginary Friends*; *Real People*; and *Only Children*. *Foreign Affairs* won the Pulitzer Prize for Fiction . in 1985.

The War between the Tates
RANDOM HOUSE, 1974

Drama. A modern comedy of manners about the academic couple Erica and Brian Tate. The war begins when Erica, a housewife, discovers that her professor husband is having an affair with his graduate student. A comic but incisive look at marriage, adolescent children, and the political turbulence of the 1960s.

LUSTBADER, ERIC VAN

Born in New York City, 1946; educated at Columbia. He has worked as a freelance writer since 1973, pursued his interest in Oriental culture, and contributed to popular music magazines. He has written *Sirens*; *Black Heart*; and the four books in the Sunset Warrior series. A recent novel is *Shan*.

The Ninja
RANDOM HOUSE, 1980

Mystery–Sex. When several bizarre murders are committed in New York City, Nicholas Linnear, of Caucasian and Oriental ancestry, knows that they must be the work of a Ninja (a legendary warrior of ancient Japan). He is asked to help the police by his medical-examiner friend and to protect a businessman who appears to be the Ninja's real target. The story moves between present-day New York, where Nicholas investigates the murders, and Japan of the 1940s and 1950s, where he grew up and learned martial arts.

Names beginning with Mc and Mac are alphabetized together.

McCLARY, JANE

Born in Pittsburgh, 1919; educated at Miss Porter's School. In addition to writing fiction she has contributed articles to magazines on skiing and horses. She has worked primarily as a journalist and won awards for journalistic achievement.

A Portion for Foxes   SIMON & SCHUSTER, 1972

Drama. Shelley Shelburn Latimer returns, with her northern newspaper husband, to her home in a unique Virginia community. Central to the story are the fox hunts, the dinner parties, and the wealth and personalities of the Valley. It is a place where outsiders are not welcomed, money does many things, and civil-rights activities are starting. Throughout the book, Shelley must grow to see things in their proper perspective—her husband, her friends, and what is morally right or wrong. The action builds from the fox hunts to a race, and finally culminates in violence.

McCULLOUGH, COLLEEN

Born in New South Wales, Australia, 1937(?); educated at the University of Sydney. She has worked as a journalist, a teacher in the Outback, a medical technician, and a director of a neurological research laboratory. She published *Tim* in 1974 and *The Ladies of Missalonghi* in 1987. A serious cook, she has also written *Cooking with Colleen McCullough and Jean Stanhope*, a guide to Australian cooking. She says, "I think of myself as a glorified typist who pounds along, chasing my characters to find out what happens."

The Thorn Birds   HARPER & ROW, 1977

Saga. In Australia, the Irish Cleary family rises from sheep shearers in the Outback to become the owners of a vast plantation. The hardships, romances, and successes of three generations of the family are shown. Change and progress are at the heart of the novel as Australia is colonized and becomes independent, and the Cleary women move from restraint to liberation.

The paperback rights for this book were sold to Avon for $1.9 million, the highest price ever at the time.

An Indecent Obsession   HARPER & ROW, 1981

War–Drama. To the battle-fatigued soldiers in Ward X, army nurse Honour Langtry is the woman they all adore and need. But when war hero and patient Michael Wilson arrives, Honour's own emotions begin to disrupt the ward's fragile security. Violence breaks out, the soldiers deal with it in their own way, and Honour must learn about the real meaning of love and duty. This is not a romance, but a skillful portrait of character and emotions.

MacDonald, John D.

Born in Pennsylvania, 1916; educated at Syracuse University and Harvard. He served in the army from 1940 to 1946, achieving the rank of lieutenant colonel. He wrote 77 books in 40 years, including many books in the Travis McGee series, each one of which has a color in the title. He was elected president of the Mystery Writers of America. His last book was *Barrier Island*. He died in 1986.

The Dreadful Lemon Sky   LIPPINCOTT, 1975

Mystery. An old friend in trouble comes to Travis and asks him to keep some money for her. Two weeks later she is dead. Travis and his friend Meyer, a world-class economist, begin asking questions. Soon they are led to a nest of corrupt politicians, a drug smuggling operation, and several other murders.

Condominium   LIPPINCOTT, 1977

Suspense. Golden Sands Condominium is built on a weak foundation— of greed, corruption, and a tie-in with organized crime. We see the lives of the various residents and the shady deals of developer Marty Liss and wait for the hurricane to strike.

The Empty Copper Sea   HARPER & ROW, 1978

Mystery. A friend of Travis is charged with negligence when the "tycoon of Timber Bay" drowns off the Florida coast. But is the man dead, and if so, is it an accident, suicide, or murder? McGee travels to Timber Bay to find the answers. Meyer and Gretel help.

The Green Ripper   HARPER & ROW, 1979

Mystery. Gretel, the woman Travis loves, thinks she has a touch of the flu and suddenly is dead from poison. So McGee must deal with his personal tragedy while he investigates this crime. He is led to a fanatic religious cult called the Church of the Apocrypha, and the Grim Reaper will claim more than one victim before the story is done.

This book won the American Book Award for Best Mystery of 1979. It was also selected by London *Times* critic H. R. F. Keating as one of the 100 best mysteries of all time (see *Crime and Mystery: The 100 Best Books*).

Free Fall in Crimson   HARPER & ROW, 1981

Mystery. Travis helps a friend investigate who killed the man's father and why the estate went to the victim's estranged wife and her filmmaker friend. The trail leads him from Florida's west coast to Beverly Hills to Iowa, where the wife and filmmaker are living off the inheritance and making a movie about hot-air balloons. Travis is still trying to recover from the loss of Gretel.

Cinnamon Skin HARPER & ROW, 1982

Mystery. Meyer's boat, the *John Maynard Keynes*, explodes, killing his niece and her husband. Or is the husband really dead? The hunt leads from New York State to Mexico and into the dark psyche of a killer. A taut story with good psychological suspense. This is the 20th book in the Travis McGee series.

MACDONALD, ROSS (PSEUDONYM OF KENNETH MILLAR)

Born in California, 1915, and reared in Canada; educated at the University of Western Ontario. He served in the navy and then received a Ph.D. from the University of Michigan. His first novel, *The Dark Tunnel* (1944), was published under his own name. He then wrote mysteries with private investigator Lew Archer as the main character, including *The Galton Case*; *The Far Side of the Dollar*; and *The Drowning Pool*. He was married to the well-known novelist Margaret Millar and served as president of the Mystery Writers of America. He died in 1983.

The Goodbye Look KNOPF, 1969

Mystery. Private detective Lew Archer is hired to investigate the theft of a gold box from a rich family, but in finding the box he stumbles upon more serious crimes both past and present. At least three murders are involved, and it appears that an emotionally disturbed young man is responsible for at least one. Archer comes to his defense as he weaves together a complex string of people and facts.

The *New York Times* reviewed this book under the title "The Finest Detective Novel Ever Written by an American." Following the *Times* review, Macdonald was catapulted from a writer with a modest number of fans to a best-selling author.

The Underground Man KNOPF, 1971

Mystery. Lew Archer attempts to find a missing little boy and runs into a forest fire and several murders, some occurring a generation before. The novel consists mainly of dialogue, Archer interviewing a number of reluctant and unhappy people, most of whom were involved in at least one of the murders.

MACINNES, HELEN

Born in Scotland, 1907; educated at the University of Glasgow and University College in London. She moved with her husband to New York City in 1937 and published her first work in 1939. Her first novel, *Above Suspicion*, was followed by many others, including *North from Rome* and *Decision at Delphi*. She died in 1985.

The Double Image HARCOURT, 1966

Spy. John Craig, a young American traveling in Paris, is drawn into a hunt for a Nazi war criminal who everyone thought was dead. The hunt takes him to the Greek island of Mykonos, where Nazis (who are also Communist agents) are plotting a new conspiracy.

The Salzburg Connection   HARCOURT, 1968

Spy. A chest buried in a lake in the Austrian Alps contains a list of men who secretly aided the Nazis and can be blackmailed into helping them again. American, Russian, and British agents all converge on Salzburg, and a young American visitor finds himself caught up in murder and intrigue.

Message from Málaga   HARCOURT, 1971

Spy. An American visits his friend in the Latin American country of Granada and soon finds himself involved in intrigue and murder. His friend, who works undercover to help Cuban refugees escape from the Communists, is in danger from Russia's infamous Department 13. Soon the American's life is in danger, too. Fortunately, he is an ex-Air Intelligence officer and can get help from the CIA.

The Snare of the Hunter   HARCOURT, 1974

International Intrigue. Irina Kusak must be escorted secretly out of Czechoslovakia to join her father, who is in hiding from the Czech Communist government. Irina's ex-husband is a part of this government, but a former lover comes forward to offer protection.

Agent in Place   HARCOURT, 1976

Spy. When a top-secret memorandum is taken and copied, agents and reporters find themselves in risky positions. A borrowed typewriter helps Tony, an English agent, get on the trail of the KGB. The action leads from Washington and New York to France, where Tony must protect another agent from the Russians and prepare for some lethal conclusions.

Prelude to Terror   HARCOURT, 1978

Spy. An art dealer is asked to go to Vienna and purchase at auction a valuable painting at any price. He quickly realizes that he is the pawn of two rival groups, each involved in secret activity and each with a beautiful female spy. Soon the art dealer joins the right side and begins dodging and trailing people like a professional. He himself may even join up when all of the violence is over.

MacLean, Alistair

Born in Scotland, 1922; he served in the Royal Navy in World War II. His first novel, *HMS Ulysses*, was based on his service experience and began his success as a writer. He worked primarily as a novelist except for a brief leave from writing in 1963 when he invested in several pubs in England. His novels, many of which were made into movies, include *Ice Station Zebra*; *The Guns of Navarone*; *When Eight Bells Toll*; and *Santorini* (1987). He died in 1987.

Where Eagles Dare   DOUBLEDAY, 1967

War. In 1944 a handful of Allied agents are sent on a seemingly impossible mission: they must rescue a general from Nazi Germany who otherwise may be forced to talk and give away the Allied plans for D-Day. Smith, one of the men on the mission, has an even more difficult task, and it cannot be completed until men have died and the treachery of double agents has been stopped.

Force 10 from Navarone   DOUBLEDAY, 1968
War. A few skilled men are sent by the Allied command into Yugoslavia to aid the partisans there. It is a suicide mission, however, into deeply occupied German territory, and none are expected to make it out.

Puppet on a Chain   DOUBLEDAY, 1969
Suspense. Major Paul Sherman, London Bureau of Interpol, Narcotics, arrives in Amsterdam with his two female assistants to receive a private message from his contact. But when his contact is murdered in front of him, there are few clues for him to follow. Then a mysterious girl at the airport leads him onto a trail of psychopathic killers, heroin addicts, and exquisite puppets, and he must kill or be killed.

Caravan to Vaccares   DOUBLEDAY, 1970
Spy. When the Gypsies arrive in the southeast of France, Neil Bowman, along with many tourists, is there to see them. But the Gypsy caravan conceals something evil and deadly, and curious Bowman wants to find out what. He claims to his female companion that he is just an "idle layabout," but when a trail of death follows Bowman, we soon learn that he and others may not be what they seem.

Bear Island   DOUBLEDAY, 1971
Mystery. A movie crew journeys by boat to Bear Island, supposedly to shoot a film. But on their way several people, both movie and boat crew personnel, die from food poisoning, and it looks to be deliberate. When they arrive at the Arctic island, more people are killed, and Dr. Marlowe wants to know who killed them and why.

Circus   DOUBLEDAY, 1975
Spy. An East European scientist has the knowledge to create antimatter that could destroy the world. When the CIA needs help in getting to the man and his scientific notes, they hire a circus performer. Bruno is the best in the world on the high wire, as well as a mentalist with a perfect photographic memory. However, when two CIA men are immediately killed, it looks as though there is a double agent in their midst.

MAILER, NORMAN

Born in New Jersey, 1923, and raised in Brooklyn; graduated from Harvard and served in the army in the Pacific. *The Naked and the Dead* (1948) was based on his experiences in the war and was followed by *Barbary Shore* and *The Deer Park*. He won a Pulitzer Prize for *The Executioner's Song* in 1979. A novel, *Ancient Evenings*, was published in 1983, and a collection of essays and interviews, *Pieces and Pontifications*, appeared in 1982.

An American Dream   DIAL PRESS, 1965
Drama. Stephen Rojack, 44, was a war hero and former congressman who once double-dated with Jack Kennedy. Rojack, however, does not grow up to be president—he undertakes a different kind of adventure.

He suddenly murders his estranged wife and plunges into an underworld of violence, magic, and organized crime. He falls in love with a
nightclub singer who is also a Mafia mistress. Courage must be shown,
secrets uncovered, and vows kept during his journey.

The Executioner's Song   LITTLE, BROWN, 1979
Drama. Mailer gives a documentary account of the Gary Gilmore case
based on actual tapes and interviews. The first half of the book shows
Gilmore, through the observations of others, in the year from his release
from prison to his arrest and conviction for murder. The second half
shows him in prison as he awaits—and demands—execution.
    The book is 1,056 pages long.

MALAMUD, BERNARD
Born in Brooklyn, 1914, of immigrant parents; educated at City College
of New York and earned an M.A. from Columbia while teaching night
classes at a high school. He has taught English at Oregon State and
Bennington, and has published collections of short stories. Some other
novels are *The Natural* (1952) and *God's Grace* (1982). He died in 1986.

The Fixer   FARRAR, STRAUS & GIROUX, 1966
Historical Novel–Religion. Yakov Bok is a Jew in Czarist Russia who
attempts to earn a living by changing his name and keeping his religion
a secret. But when a Christian boy is murdered, the officials need a
scapegoat so they can start a pogrom. They arrest Yakov and attempt
to break his spirit and that of all the other Jews in the country.
    This novel won a National Book Award and a Pulitzer Prize.

Dubin's Lives   FARRAR, STRAUS & GIROUX, 1979
Drama. William Dubin is a biographer who learns from others' lives,
but his own is not going well. He cannot begin his biography of Lawrence, or love his wife, or deal with his obsession for 22-year-old Fanny.
Malamud gives us a wryly comic account of his hero, as Dubin jogs and
goes on diets, and looks to the words of his own biographies to wrest a
solution.

MARSHALL, CATHERINE
Born in Tennessee, 1914. The widow of U.S. Senate Chaplain Peter
Marshall, she wrote the biography *A Man Called Peter*, which became a
nonfiction best seller. She wrote other religious books for children and
adults and, with her second husband, founded Chosen Books, a publishing company specializing in inspirational works. *Christy*, based on her
mother's experiences as a teacher, was her first novel. She died in 1983.

Christy   MCGRAW, 1967
Historical Novel–Religion. Nineteen-year-old Christy leaves her com-
fortable home in 1912 to teach the poor children of Appalachia in
eastern Tennessee. The book shows a year in her life there and the
crisis of faith that she and other characters must face. Many pages of
religious discourse are included with the narrative.

MERRICK, GORDON

Born in Pennsylvania, 1916; educated at Princeton. He has been an actor, journalist, and television writer as well as a novelist. His first novel was *The Strumpet Wind*, a story about World War II. He has also written *The Vallency Tradition* and *The Hot Season*.

The Lord Won't Mind   BERNARD GEIS, 1970

Drama-Sex. A story of homosexual love. Charles and Peter are brought together by Charles's grandmother, C. B., and begin a passionate physical affair. But their relationship is affected by Charles's domination by his bizarre grandmother, his marriage to a woman, and Peter's search for his own independence and maturity.

MEYER, NICHOLAS

Born in New York City, 1945; educated at the University of Iowa, where he received an M.B.A in theatre and film. He writes screenplays, including one for *The Seven-Per-Cent Solution*, and has directed films such as *Time after Time* and *Star Trek II*. In addition to his two best sellers, he also wrote *Target Practice* and *Confessions of a Homing Pigeon*.

The Seven-Per-Cent Solution   DUTTON, 1974

Mystery–Historical Novel. The story opens with Sherlock Holmes seriously addicted to cocaine and under the illusion that a Professor Moriarty is an arch-fiend. Loyal Watson, seeing the urgency of Holmes's situation, tricks him into seeing a doctor world renowned for aiding people with mental problems. Thus begins Holmes's brief but fruitful friendship with Dr. Sigmund Freud, as they join together to solve a case.

Meyer approaches this book as merely the editor of "author" John H. Watson's reminiscences.

The West End Horror   DUTTON, 1976

Mystery–Historical Novel. Sherlock Holmes and Watson investigate murders occurring in the theatre district of London. The motive, however, remains hidden until they finally hear the doomed murderer's confession. In the course of their investigation they encounter such people as Bernard Shaw, Gilbert and Sullivan, Bram Stoker, and Oscar Wilde.

Once again Meyer poses as the editor of Watson's manuscripts.

MICHENER, JAMES

He was discovered as a foundling in New York City, and he gives his official record of birth as 1907; he went on to gain a scholarship to Swarthmore, and then served in the navy in the South Pacific. His *Tales of the South Pacific* won a Pulitzer Prize and was made into the musical *South Pacific*, and *Centennial* became a television miniseries, which he narrated. In the course of his career, Michener has donated a large part of his royalty income for scholarships to young writers and artists. He was awarded the President's Medal of Freedom for fiction. He has recently published *Texas* and *Legacy,* and looks forward to a book on the Caribbean and "a good football novel."

The Source   RANDOM HOUSE, 1965

Religion–Historical Novel. Artifacts found at the fictional site of Makor hold 12,000 years of history—all the way from the cave dwellers to the Hebrew kings to the founders of the modern state of Israel. Working with 15 artifacts and 15 layers of history, Michener has a story for each, telling of the gods who are worshipped and the blood that is spilled in their name. In the process, he reconstructs the development of Western religious thought and the conflicts that continue to the present day.

The Drifters   RANDOM HOUSE, 1971

Drama. A sympathetic look at the youth culture at the end of the 1960s. The story follows six young people as they travel in Europe and Africa: an idealistic draft evader, a black militant, a folk singer from a proper Bostonian family, and others. Michener gives a full account of their lives and problems along with a colorful tour of the places they visit.

Centennial   RANDOM HOUSE, 1974

Historical Novel. The fictional town of Centennial, Colorado, is the setting for this novel. Michener creates a complete history of the town beginning with the formation of the Rocky Mountains and proceeding chapter by chapter to the dinosaurs, other animals, the Indians, the settlers, and current residents. While the story ends in the 1970s, the majority of the action takes place in the second half of the 19th century.

Chesapeake   RANDOM HOUSE, 1978

Historical Novel–Saga. The main action occurs on Maryland's eastern shore. It covers 400 years, starting with the founding fathers who came there to seek refuge from persecution and following their descendants through the centuries. A unifying theme is provided by the voyages that precede each chapter as the characters arrive at Chesapeake.

The Covenant   RANDOM HOUSE, 1980

Historical Novel–Saga. Five hundred years of South African history are captured by three fictional families—one African, one Afrikaner, and one English. The families interact with each other through the years, in cooperation and conflict, but the seeds are being sown for the modern problem of race and the horrors of apartheid.

Space   RANDOM HOUSE, 1982

Drama–American Politics. Fast-moving narrative makes this one of the best of the Michener stories. The author gives a panoramic and human picture of the space program, focusing on four families from the project's beginning in the late 1940s through to the 1980s. We see the training of the astronauts, the deals made in congressional committee, the pressures on men and women from public relations, and the debates on the direction of the program.

Poland   RANDOM HOUSE, 1983

Historical Novel–Saga. A wide-ranging view of the history and spirit of Poland from the Tatar invasion through the Nazi occupation to the troubles of the present day. Broad historical strokes are combined with careful detail as Michener traces three families through eight centuries: the noble Lubonskis, the Bukowskis of the gentry, and the peasant Buks.

MIDLER, BETTE

Born in Honolulu, 1945; educated at the University of Hawaii and Hunter College. She is an actress and recording artist, and starred in the movie *The Rose* and the Broadway production of *Fiddler on the Roof.* Her talents have earned her an Emmy and two Grammy awards. Her first book was *A View from a Broad.*

The Saga of Baby Divine   CROWN, 1983

Drama. Told in poetic form. When Baby Divine is born with red hair and wearing high heels, her parents think there must be a mistake. But Lily, Tillie, and Joyce, who used to perform on stage, know that a special baby has been born. So when Baby Divine dances out into the night, the three women are there to save her from the dreadful Anxiety and set her on the road to entertainment.

Illustrated by Todd Schorr, whose work has been on the covers of major magazines.

MOORE, ROBIN (PSEUDONYM OF ROBERT LOWELL MOORE)

Born in Massachusetts, 1925; educated at Harvard. He participated each year in Green Beret training missions and helped to compose "The Ballad of the Green Berets." He is also the author of *The French Connection.*

The Green Berets   CROWN, 1965

War. Moore describes several missions of different teams of the Special Forces, showing us the diverse men who fought the war, its effect on them and on the civilian population. Throughout the book, the author shows the efficient operation of the Special Forces, creating the impression that the United States would win the battle against Communism in Vietnam. But this book was published in 1965, before the losses of the next several years, the large-scale protests on the home front, and ultimate withdrawal from Vietnam.

The author trained with the Green Berets as a civilian, and journeyed to Vietnam to gather information for this story. Based on fact, it was fictionalized only to protect individual and national rights.

MYDANS, SHELLEY

Born in California, 1915. She worked as a journalist, a reporter for *Life* magazine and a correspondent covering Europe and the Far East. She was a prisoner of war of the Japanese in World War II, and wrote the book *The Open City* based on this experience. She is also the author of the historical novel *The Vermillion Bridge.*

Thomas   DOUBLEDAY, 1965
Historical Novel–Religion. The life of Thomas à Becket, 12th-century political and religious leader, set against the background of England at the time. Thomas, born a commoner, rises to become chancellor and friend to the king, and ultimately the archbishop. He learns early how to compromise in matters between the church and the state. But when he finally must choose between his faith and the king, no compromises are possible.

MYRER, ANTON

Born in Massachusetts, 1922; educated at Harvard. He typically writes of Massachusetts settings, and his novels include *The Last Convertible* and *The Tiger Waits*.

A Green Desire   PUTNAM, 1982
Drama. Two brothers take different paths on their way to adulthood. One chooses to live with his aunt and be brought up in luxury, while the other stays with his mother and remains poor. But their paths continue to cross as they compete for the same woman, gain wealth and success on Wall Street, and suffer loss and the threat of death.

NABOKOV, VLADIMIR VLADIMIROVICH

Born in Russia, 1899, to an aristocratic family. He published a volume of poetry before he and his family were forced to leave in 1919. He studied French and Russian literature at Trinity College, Cambridge, then lived in Berlin and Paris and wrote in Russian under the pseudonym Sirin. Nabokov moved to the United States in 1940 and became an American citizen in 1945. He was a lecturer at Wellesley College and a professor of Russian literature at Cornell until 1959. After his success with *Lolita*, he left teaching to write full-time and moved to Switzerland. He died in 1977. His book *The Enchanter* was published posthumously.

Ada or Ardor   MCGRAW, 1969
Drama–Sex. The story of Dr. Ivan (Van) Veen, psychologist and philosopher of time, and his lifelong love for his half-sister Ada. Nabokov's eroticism and plays with language are sustained throughout the novel.

NIN, ANAÏS (PRONOUNCED "NEEN")

Born in France, 1903; she moved to the United States at the age of 11, and left school at 15. Best known for *The Diaries of Anaïs Nin*, she also wrote critical books, short stories, and such novels as *The Four-Chambered Heart* and *A Spy in the House of Love*. She died in 1977.

Delta of Venus: Erotica   HARCOURT, 1977
Short Stories–Sex. The 15 very short tales included here are a kind of feminine *Decameron*. Nin attempts to show sexual experience from a woman's point of view, entering the field of erotic writing previously known only to men. The stories, marked by great physical power, poetry, and some humor, show a variety of situations: the Hungarian adven-

turer and his daughters; the two boys in the Jesuit school; the cold wife who believes she has been given Spanish fly by her husband; and the woman with two lovers—one for day and one for night.

O'CONNOR, EDWIN

Born in Rhode Island, 1918; educated at the University of Notre Dame. His first novel was *The Oracle* (1951), which was followed by *The Last Hurrah*; *The Edge of Sadness*; and *I Was Dancing*. He won a Pulitzer Prize in 1962, and died in 1968.

All in the Family   LITTLE, BROWN, 1966

American Politics. In *The Last Hurrah* O'Connor wrote about old-style machine politics. Here he turns to the new politics—Kennedy-style. The story is of the Kinsellas, a well-to-do Irish family in Massachusetts, and the effects of political corruption. One brother runs for governor, cheered on by the other family members and especially the magnificent "Uncle Jimmy." But the old politics engulfs the new, pitting brother against brother and causing the ultimate breakup of the family unit.

O'HARA, JOHN

Born in Pennsylvania, 1905. He wrote numerous books, including *Butterfield 8*; *Appointment in Samarra*; and *From the Terrace*, and also short stories and plays. He received the National Book Award for *Ten North Frederick* and an Award of Merit for his novels from the American Academy of Arts and Letters in 1964. He died in 1970. Critic Sheldon Grebstein observed that future readers will return to O'Hara "to find out how it was to live in the first half of the twentieth century" (*Contemporary Authors*).

The Horse Knows the Way   RANDOM HOUSE, 1964

Short Stories. With brief scenes and realistic dialogue, O'Hara captures a range of characters, all ordinary but fairly unpleasant people. Four of the 28 stories first appeared in the *New Yorker*, and 13 in the *Saturday Evening Post*.

The Lockwood Concern   RANDOM HOUSE, 1965

Saga. Abraham Lockwood and his son George care about only one thing—establishing a family dynasty in their small Pennsylvania town. When George's family refuses to go along with the plan, he must carry on the Concern for himself.

Waiting for Winter   RANDOM HOUSE, 1966

Short Stories. Ten were previously published elsewhere (the *New Yorker*, the *Saturday Evening Post*, *Sports Illustrated*), and 11 are new. O'Hara's dialogue carries the action in these taut, often downbeat stories. Many of the characters are old, have lost something, or are waiting for death.

The Instrument   RANDOM HOUSE, 1967

Drama. A study of gifted playwright Yank Lucas, who feels passion only for his work. The other characters in the story help to show Yank's emotional impotence: he uses them only as a means to gain his own ends. Yank writes two plays in the course of the novel, and at one point his life is saved. Others, however, do not fare as well.

And Other Stories   RANDOM HOUSE, 1968

Short Stories. A collection of 11 short stories and one novella, four of which first appeared in the *Saturday Evening Post* and one in the *New Yorker*. The stories are primarily character sketches of ordinary people, and O'Hara takes us beneath the surface to see what they are really like. In the Foreword, the author says of short stories, "No one writes them better than I do."

PATTERSON, HARRY (JACK HIGGINS)

Born in England, 1929; educated at the London School of Economics. He served with the Royal Horse Guards from 1947 to 1950. A prolific writer, he has published under five pen names altogether, and his daughter published a successful novel at the age of 16. *Night of the Fox* appeared in 1987 under the name of Jack Higgins.

The Eagle Has Landed   HOLT, 1975

War. In World War II, a small band of German paratroopers lands on the Norfolk coast with the aim of capturing Churchill, who is visiting there. The Germans are portrayed as ordinary soldiers, capable of weakness, heroism, and humanity, in this tale of adventure and suspense.

The Valhalla Exchange   STEIN & DAY, 1976

War. In the closing days of World War II, Nazi leader Martin Bormann attempts to use five Allied prisoners as hostages to secure his escape. The Allies fight back, although they are outnumbered and overpowered, and at least one of them may be a Nazi agent in disguise.

Storm Warning   HOLT, 1976

War. In 1944 a 19th-century sailing vessel called the *Deutschland* sails from Brazil, with 22 crewmen and five nuns aboard, in an attempt to go home to Germany. Meanwhile, an American doctor, a German U-boat hero, and various Englishmen, Scots, and Germans are also contributing efforts to the war. When the *Deutschland* founders in a storm off the coast of Scotland, they all come together and take action that transcends their enmities. Written under the name Jack Higgins.

Not to be confused with an event in 1875 when a real ship called the *Deutschland* perished with five nuns aboard. Gerard Manley Hopkins wrote a poem, "The Wreck of the Deutschland," about the 1875 event.

PEARSON, DREW

Born in Illinois, 1897; educated at Phillips Academy and Swarthmore. Pearson worked as a journalist and Washington correspondent, and wrote the syndicated column "Washington Merry-Go-Round" from 1931 to 1969. As correspondent, he attended the Paris Peace Conference of 1946 and subsequent summit conferences, and interviewed Premier Khrushchev, President Tito, and the king and queen of Greece. He died in 1969.

The Senator　　　　　　　　　　　　　　　　　　DOUBLEDAY, 1968
American Politics. The story of Senator Benjamin Hannaford as told
by his admiring aide Edward Deever. Hannaford, a power in the Senate
and autocrat in committee, is heavily involved in bribery and conflict of
interest. A crusading journalist, Lou Parenti, plays a part in the ultimate
investigation of Hannaford's crimes.

　　　Pearson published a nonfiction book, *The Case against Congress* (coauthored with Jack Anderson) in the same year. The *Senator* is a fictional
rendition of this case.

PERCY, WALKER

　　　Born in Alabama, 1916; educated at the University of North Carolina,
and received an M.D. from Columbia. He gave up medicine because of
his own bad health. His first novel, *The Moviegoer*, won a National Book
Award in 1961. He has also written *The Last Gentleman* and its sequel,
The Second Coming.

Love in the Ruins　　　　　　　　　FARRAR, STRAUS & GIROUX, 1971
Science Fiction—Religion. The time is the future, when cars do not work,
vines grow in Manhattan, and rival groups battle one another. Dr.
Thomas More, however, has developed a "stethoscope of the spirit"
which can diagnose all the secret ills, depressions, and terrors that beset
the human race. If only he could cure what he can diagnose . . . or at
least cure his own spiritual ills.

　　　Percy subtitled this book *The Adventures of a Bad Catholic at a Time
near the End of the World*. The satire has some warm optimistic notes.

PETRAKIS, HARRY

　　　Born in St. Louis, 1923; educated at the University of Illinois. He has
worked as a teacher and lecturer. He is the author of the novels *Lion
at My Heart* and *The Odyssey of Kostas Volakis*, and the collection of short
stories *Pericles on 31st St.* That collection and *A Dream of Kings* were both
nominated for a National Book Award.

A Dream of Kings　　　　　　　　　　　　　　DAVID MCKAY, 1966
Drama. Leonidas Matsoukas fights, loves, and gambles joyously and runs
the Pindar Counseling Service (solutions provided for all problems of
life and love). He attempts to save his money to bring his tragically ill
son back to Greece, where he feels the sun will revive him. Heroic and
larger than life, but very human at times, Matsoukas must do battle with
the gods to save his son.

The Waves of Night and Other Stories　　　　　DAVID MCKAY, 1969
Short Stories. This book collects 10 short stories and one novella, some
of which have appeared in *Playboy*, *U.S. Catholic*, and other magazines,
and others of which were previously unpublished. Petrakis continues
to write about the Greek-American experience with a mixture of bra-
vado and despair. "The Waves of Night" recounts one week in the life
of a Greek priest tormented by his loss of faith. "Rosemary" tells about

an encounter between a lunchroom owner and a customer, and "The Bastards of Thanos" shows an unrepentant sinner who finds his own kind of redemption before death.

PLAIN, BELVA

Born in New York City, 1919(?); educated at Barnard College. She has published numerous short stories in addition to the books *Crescent City* and *The Golden Cup*.

Evergreen   DELACORTE, 1978

Saga. Anna is a Polish Jewish immigrant who comes to America; she rises from poverty to raise a family and carry on a lifelong romance. The story covers three generations, and the romances, births, and deaths of the various family members from the turn of the century to the 1970s.

Random Winds   DELACORTE, 1980

Saga. The story encompasses three generations of doctors, but focuses chiefly on Martin (of the second generation) and his lifelong love for his sister-in-law Mary Fern.

Eden Burning   DELACORTE, 1982

Saga. Two generations of the Francis family and their island estate on St. Felice are shown in this story. The tale includes marriages, divorce, domestic friction, children, a rape, and an assassination.

PLATH, SYLVIA

Born in Massachusetts, 1932. She started writing at an early age, and while a student at Smith College was published in *Seventeen* and *Mademoiselle*. Plath married British poet Ted Hughes, and taught in the English Department at Smith College. After years of mental illness, she committed suicide in 1963. Her only novel was *The Bell Jar*, but she is known mainly for her poetry. Her *Collected Poems* won a Pulitzer Prize in 1982.

The Bell Jar   HARPER & ROW, 1971

Drama. Autobiographical novel of a young girl who wins a job on a New York magazine, and her subsequent mental breakdown and suicide attempt. It is a detailed look, both comic and painful, at the world from the point of view of a person fighting for identity and life.

This novel was published about eight years after Plath's death.

PORTIS, CHARLES

Born in Arkansas, 1933; educated at the University of Arkansas, then served in the Marine Corps. He has worked as a reporter and London correspondent for the *New York Herald Tribune*. Other novels are *Norwood* and *The Dog of the South*.

True Grit   SIMON & SCHUSTER, 1968

Western–Historical Novel. When her father is murdered, 14-year-old Mattie Ross is determined to avenge his death. She convinces Rooster Cogburn, a U.S. marshal, to help her track down the murderer, who has joined a band of outlaws. Together they ride out into the dangerous Indian territory, both showing their "true grit." The novel gives a comic and warm-hearted view of this unusual pair.

POTOK, CHAIM

Born in New York City, 1929, to Orthodox Jewish parents; he graduated from Yeshiva University and the Jewish Theological Seminary of America, was ordained as a rabbi, and has a Ph.D. in philosophy. He served as an army chaplain during the Korean War. Potok is the editor of the Jewish Publication Society of America, and has written the novel *The Book of Lights* and the nonfiction *Wanderings: Chaim Potok's Personal History of the Jews.*

The Chosen   SIMON & SCHUSTER, 1967

Drama–Religion. Psychological portraits of two boys growing up in Brooklyn in the 1940s, their rivalry, friendship, and search for a moral identity. Their conflicts are heightened and paralleled by those of their fathers—one a Hasidic rabbi and one a more worldly scholar.

The Promise   KNOPF, 1969

Drama–Religion. This is the sequel to *The Chosen.* Now the boys are young men, and they both are struggling in the beginnings of their careers. Reuven Malter, the scholar's son, is studying to be a rabbi, but he is challenged by his teacher, Rav Kalman. Danny Saunders is starting out as a clinical psychologist, but many find him controversial in his techniques. Both men must take great risks as they gamble on their futures.

My Name Is Asher Lev   KNOPF, 1972

Drama. Asher Lev grows up with a genius and compulsion to paint. His parents, however, are strict Jewish Hasidim who frown on art and who are themselves engrossed in the work of freeing Jewish refugees from Russia. Asher proceeds with his painting, with the blessing of the Rebbe and help from his mother, but the conflict continues and grows as he paints nudes and crucifixions. Finally, a painting and a triumphant exhibition mark the crucial turning point away from his parents' world and his past.

In the Beginning   KNOPF, 1975

Drama–Religion. The story of David Lurie and his Orthodox religious family from the 1920s to the 1940s. David grows up in the Bronx, beset by illnesses and persecution against Jews. His parents, active in an organization that brings people to America, suffer throughout the Depression and the horror of the Holocaust. But this is a book about beginnings—and David must make his own as he searches for truth and decides to become a biblical scholar.

PRICE, EUGENIA

Born in West Virginia, 1916; educated at Ohio University. She has written fiction and nonfiction, including religious and autobiographical works. She has recently published the historical novel *Before the Darkness Falls*.

New Moon Rising   LIPPINCOTT, 1969

Historical Novel. A story of a family in 19th-century Georgia. In this sequel to *The Beloved Invader*, Horace Gould grows up, begins to oversee the cotton plantation, and marries the simple, but fruitful, Deborah. As the Civil War approaches, he feels conflicting loyalties, but joins the Confederate army. Horace watches with growing anguish as his lands are ravaged and given over to strangers.

Price says in the acknowledgment that the characters are based on real people and were drawn from interviews, biographies, and other historical records.

PUZO, MARIO

Born in Hell's Kitchen on Manhattan's West Side, 1920; educated at the New School for Social Research and Columbia University. He served in the air force in Germany in World War II. His first books, *The Fortunate Pilgrim* and *Dark Arena*, brought him critical acclaim. He won two Oscars for the films *Godfather* and *Godfather II*, and also wrote the screenplays for *Earthquake*; *Superman*; and *Superman II*. He wrote the spy novel *Six Graves to Munich* under the pseudonym Mario Cleri, and also published an illustrated nonfiction book called *Inside Las Vegas*.

The Godfather   PUTNAM, 1969

Drama. Epic tale of an organized-crime family headed by Don Vito Corleone, its mores and ways of doing business. The tale encompasses both warm family loyalty, marriages, and children, and ruthless power, betrayal, and murder. In the course of the story, we see the decline of the family until the youngest son, Michael, rises up to head the syndicate.

Fools Die   PUTNAM, 1978

Drama. Fiction writer and part-time petty criminal John Merlyn seeks magic and adventure in contemporary America with a small circle of friends. The action ranges from Las Vegas gambling casinos to suburban Long Island, while the unique characters are drawn larger than life. As author Puzo says at the beginning, it's a story about friendship and loyalty, passionate living, love and death.

The Sicilian   SIMON & SCHUSTER, 1984

Adventure. In Sicily, Salvatore Guiliano and his friend Aspanu Pisciotta fight and rob the corrupt rich and help the peasants. Salvatore is a hero to most of Sicily, but he has made enemies with Don Croce Malo, the head of the "Friends of the Friends." Michael Corleone has been ordered to find Guiliano and bring him back to America, and Michael will not be allowed to return without him.

RAUCHER, HERMAN

Born in Brooklyn, 1928; educated at New York University. He served in the army from 1950 to 1952, then worked for 20th Century Fox

Films and Walt Disney Studios. He wrote the novels *Ode to Billy Joe*; *Watermelon Man*; and *Sweet November*, and has also written screenplays.

Summer of '42 PUTNAM, 1971

Drama. A middle-aged man returns to an island off the New England coast and recalls the summer of 1942, when he and his two friends were 15. The boys were preoccupied with sex—they talked about it, read about it, and began to try and practice it. The narrator's memories evoke all the details and nostalgia of the time, including a one-night affair with a woman whose husband had just been killed in the war. Raucher wrote the script for the movie before he wrote the novel.

RENAULT, MARY (PSEUDONYM OF MARY CHALLANS)

Born in England, 1905; educated at Oxford. Trained as a classicist, she became known for the extensive research she brought to each of her historical novels. She achieved fame with *The King Must Die* (1958) and *The Bull from the Sea* (1962). She died in 1983.

The Mask of Apollo RANDOM HOUSE, 1966

Historical Novel. In the 4th century B.C., the Greek city of Syracuse is under the rule of tyranny and torn by strife. When Plato and Dion, advisers to the petulant young king Dionysius, try to bring reforms, they only hasten the building conflict and downfall of the city. The events are seen by the central character and narrator, the very likable actor Nikeratos. He tells of the actor's craft at the time: the traveling, techniques, and the way the cast and plays are selected. But as he rises to become a leading tragic actor, he is drawn into the real-world tragedy occurring around him.

Most of the characters are historical figures, except Nikeratos, who is the author's own creation.

Fire from Heaven RANDOM HOUSE, 1969

Historical Novel. Basing her account on Plutarch and other historical sources, Renault tells the story of Alexander the Great from childhood to age 20, when he succeeded to the throne. We are shown Alexander's great friendship with Hephaistion and the complex character of his father, King Philip of Macedon, as well as the military and political events of the time.

The Persian Boy RANDOM HOUSE, 1972

Historical Novel. The last years and conquests of Alexander the Great are recounted by the young slave boy Bagoas, who loves him. Bagoas tells of Alexander's need for affection and his small idiosyncrasies, as well as his sense of destiny and great ambition. The book follows Alexander's conquests from Persia through India and finally to Babylonia, with their long marches, discipline, and human encounters. It is Bagoas's story, too, in his worship of Alexander and growing skill in diplomacy and court politics. Renault supplies a detailed account of her historical sources at the end of the book. Bagoas was a real person.

RIVERS, JOAN (PROFESSIONAL NAME OF JOAN MOLINSKY)

Born in New York City, 1937; educated at Barnard College. She was a fashion coordinator for Bond Clothing Stores, and a syndicated columnist for the *Chicago Tribune*. Rivers has also been an actress, writer, and director in films, and has been featured as a television personality.

The Life and Hard Times of Heidi Abromowitz   DELACORTE, 1984
Drama–Sex. A comic view of the life of a tramp, from Baby Bimbo Abromowitz to the Broad Abroad to Hooker Housewife. Told through a series of one-liners, it even includes a quiz to test the reader's own "Tramp Potential."

ROBBINS, HAROLD

Born Francis Kane in New York City, 1916, he was adopted at the age of 11 and given the name Harold Robbins. He became a millionaire by the age of 20 from work in the food industry, and later lost his money, becoming a shipping clerk with Universal Pictures. He became an executive director at Universal within two years and went on to a career as a best-selling novelist. His first novel, *Never Love a Stranger*, the story of an orphan, is considered heavily autobiographical. Other novels include *The Carpetbaggers*; *The Dream Merchants*; *Piranha*; and *The Storyteller*.

The Adventurers   SIMON & SCHUSTER, 1966
International Intrigue–Glamour–Sex. Chronicle of Diogenes Alejandro Xenos, a South American who goes to Harvard. The action combines international finance, Latin American revolution, polo, high fashion, and many sexual adventures.

The Inheritors   SIMON & SCHUSTER, 1969
Glamour–Sex. Stephen Gaunt takes over as president of Sinclair Broadcasting Company and brings it to the top of the ratings. He has status, money, and so many women that he must give them nicknames to keep them straight (Blonde Girl, Lawyer Girl, Chinese Girl). As part of his adventures, he betrays a friend, tries to buy him back, and helps in the destruction of the friend's daughter.

The Betsy   SIMON & SCHUSTER, 1971
Sex–Drama. The Betsy is a car of tomorrow as dreamed by Loren Hardeman, head of Bethlehem Motors. When racing-car driver Angelo Perini is asked to build it, he is caught up in the Hardeman family strife. Conflicts involve the grandfather, who is called Number One, a weak son, a grandson who fights his grandfather with his own ruthless business practices, and a granddaughter named Betsy.

The Pirate   SIMON & SCHUSTER, 1974
International Intrigue–Sex. Baydr Samir Al Fay is one of the richest men in the world, investing in Western business to make more money for his Arabian homeland. He steers his course through international intrigue and the activities of revolutionary groups, and appears invincible until his daughter joins the revolutionaries and his sons are kidnapped by them.

The Lonely Lady   SIMON & SCHUSTER, 1976
  Glamour–Sex. The life and hard times of JeriLee Randall, including
  an abortion, a rape, exploitation by film producers and other men, and
  commitment to a detoxification center. JeriLee, however, wants to be a
  writer and remain independent. When she finally succeeds, in the epi-
  logue to the novel, she takes her revenge at an Academy Awards ceremony.

Dreams Die First   SIMON & SCHUSTER, 1977
  Drama–Sex. An out-of-work writer and ex–Green Beret finds himself
  in debt to a Hollywood crime syndicate. He begins to work for them by
  publishing a pornographic newspaper with the help of his Chicano girlfriend, a homosexual, and a member of a religious cult. From there he
  goes on to build a net worth of millions, but his fortune and life remain
  at risk in a world of drugs, hard-core sex, and organized crime.

Memories of Another Day   SIMON & SCHUSTER, 1979
  Drama. Young Jonathan is glad that his father is dead, but soon strange
  feelings and memories begin to haunt him. His father grew up in rural
  poverty to become a powerful union leader—tough enough to survive
  threats and beatings, and to give out some of his own. But Big Dan
  needs something from his youngest son, and not even death can stand
  in the way.

Goodbye, Janette   SIMON & SCHUSTER, 1981
  Glamour–Sex–Drama. Tanya, a survivor of a Nazi concentration camp,
  makes a liaison that ensures her survival and fortune. Her daughter,
  Janette, makes a match for convenience, too—with her mother's brutally
  sadistic former lover. Janette goes on to found a famous house of fashion
  and engage in a wide variety of sexual adventures, many of them involving whips.

ROSSNER, JUDITH
  Born in New York City, 1935; educated at City College of New York.
  She has been divorced twice. In addition to her many novels, she has
  also written short stories. Novels include *To the Precipice* (1966), *Attach-
  ments* (1977), and *Emmeline* (1980).

Looking for Mr. Goodbar   SIMON & SCHUSTER, 1975
  Drama–Sex. A young woman is killed by a pickup she makes in a singles
  bar. Rossner traces her life, and the men she had known, to that point.
  Her character is a schoolteacher, an invalid as a child, who is basically
  unhappy and does not know why. The book was inspired by a real-life
  murder on Manhattan's Upper West Side. Rossner weaves a complex
  psychological portrait from the bare facts.

August   HOUGHTON MIFFLIN, 1983
  Drama–Sex. The story of Dawn Henley, 18, the victim of a disastrous
  childhood, and her psychoanalyst, Dr. Lulu Scheinfeld, twice divorced
  and in her forties. The novel traces their parallel lives and their relationship.

ROTH, PHILIP

Born in New Jersey, 1933; educated at Bucknell and the University of Chicago. He served in the army from 1955 to 1956. He has taught English and creative writing and was the writer in residence at the University of Pennsylvania from 1965 to 1980. Roth received a National Book Award for Fiction in 1960 and an American Book Award (declined) in 1980 for *The Ghostwriter*. Many of his novels deal with the same main character, a Jewish novelist: *My Life as a Man*; *Zuckerman Unbound*; and *The Anatomy Lesson*, among others. He has also written a story about baseball (*The Great American Novel*) and has recently published *The Counterlife* and an autobiography, *The Facts*.

When She Was Good   RANDOM HOUSE, 1967

Drama. Portrait of young Lucy Nelson, who hates her father, feels contemptuous of others, and tries to cling to her own moral superiority. Roth shows us the obsessed personality from the inside: Lucy wants to control others and to find someone who will be in control.

Portnoy's Complaint   RANDOM HOUSE, 1969

Drama–Sex. Chronicle of the life of Alexander Portnoy, as told by a psychiatrist. Portnoy has a dominating mother, a father he cannot respect, and an all-embracing sense of Jewish guilt. He masturbates compulsively, in all ways and places. We follow his difficulties through achievements at Columbia Law School, his work as a lawyer for a congressional committee, and his relations with a series of women.

Our Gang   RANDOM HOUSE, 1971

American Politics. Political satire of the Nixon presidency. The theme is the use and abuse of words to create lies and deception; and the narrative takes Trick E. Dixon through press conferences and planning sessions in the White House, then to his comeback and assassination, when he runs for the office of Devil in Hell. In capturing the clichés and rhythms of presidential rhetoric, the book goes beyond any one administration or individual in office.

RUARK, ROBERT

Born in 1915. He was a commissioned officer in World War II, was a famous journalist and war correspondent, and later became a syndicated columnist. He lived abroad in Africa, Spain, and London. Two of his novels, *Something of Value* and *Uhuru*, have African settings. He died in 1965.

The Honey Badger   MANUSCRIPTS, INC., 1965

Drama–Sex. At age 42, Alex Barr is a successful writer and journalist when he leaves his marriage and begins a series of affairs. Along the way he recounts, at great length, his past exploits—in the navy, in college, and on hunting expeditions. But when he becomes ill at age 49, he must choose between his manhood and his life.

The author died before the book was published, and it is considered at least partly autobiographical. The negative stereotypes of women and homosexuals will offend many readers.

SAFIRE, WILLIAM

Born in New York City, 1929; educated at Syracuse University. He served in the army from 1952 to 1954. He has worked as a reporter, correspondent, and producer for radio and television, and was special assistant to President Nixon. He has been a columnist for the *New York Times* since 1973, and won a Pulitzer Prize for Distinguished Commentary in 1978. Safire also writes nonfiction books on politics, including *Safire's Political Dictionary* and *Freedom*.

Full Disclosure   DOUBLEDAY, 1977
American Politics. What happens if the president appears to be unable to perform his duties? Safire raises a real political question in this tale of a blinded president, a coverup, an ambitious cabinet member, and loyal and disloyal staff. In the process, we get an inside look at the strategies and procedures of those who work in the White House.

ST. JOHNS, ADELA

Born in California, 1894. She worked as a reporter and feature writer for the *Los Angeles Herald* and International News Service, and became known (according to *Contemporary Authors*) as "the world's greatest girl reporter" in the 1930s. While she covered politics and sports as well as other subjects, she was best known for her inside stories of Hollywood. She left journalism in the 1950s to write short stories, novels, and many screenplays full-time. *The Honeycomb* and *Love, Laughter, and Tears* are autobiographical works.

Tell No Man   DOUBLEDAY, 1966
Religion. Chicago investment specialist Hank Gavin has a sudden religious awakening that leads him to enter the ministry. The book then recounts his experiences as a pastor, with excerpts from sermons and religious discussion. Hank must try to build a church and survive a chilling crisis of faith.

The writing in this book is so poor as to make it difficult to read.

SALINGER, PIERRE

Born in San Francisco, 1925; educated at the University of San Francisco. He served in the navy from 1942 to 1945. Salinger worked as a reporter and editor for the *San Francisco Chronicle*, served as press secretary to Presidents Kennedy and Johnson, and was an ambassador and a senator from California. Since 1977, he has worked for ABC News as a foreign correspondent. He coauthored *The Dossier* (1984) with Leonard Gross.

On Instructions of My Government   DOUBLEDAY, 1971
American Politics–International Intrigue. The Chinese attempt to establish a long-range missile base in the Latin American country of Santa

Clara. We see the president's handling of the crisis and the conflicts facing U.S. ambassador Sam Hood. Confronted with what he sees as a potential disaster in policy, Hood must balance claims of career and judgment and decide what his own role in the crisis will be.

Since Salinger was press secretary during the Cuban Missile Crisis, the exchanges in the novel between president and press secretary are especially worth reading.

SANDERS, LAWRENCE

Born in Brooklyn, 1920; educated at Wabash College, then served in the Marine Corps from 1943 to 1946. He was an editor at *Mechanix Illustrated* and *Science and Mechanics*, and freelanced for other magazines. Sanders become a novelist in 1969, and recently published *The Timothy Files* (1987).

The First Deadly Sin　　　　　　　　　　　　　　　　PUTNAM, 1973

Mystery. The first deadly sin is pride. Sanders gives parallel stories of a very human cop and a disturbed killer, as Captain Edward X. Delaney hunts down David Blank and comes to question his own moral pride and loss of compassion.

The Second Deadly Sin　　　　　　　　　　　　　　　PUTNAM, 1977

Mystery. The second deadly sin is greed. Victor Maitland was a great artist but a terrible human being, and many people stood to gain by his death. All of the suspects have motives of greed, but which one is guilty of murder? Ex–chief of detectives Delaney investigates.

The Sixth Commandment　　　　　　　　　　　　　　PUTNAM, 1979

Mystery. An investigator for the Bingham Foundation starts a routine check on a famous doctor's application for a million-dollar grant. He soon finds himself led to a remote clinic where lethal experiments are carried out and bodies are buried in the dead of night.

The Third Deadly Sin　　　　　　　　　　　　　　　PUTNAM, 1981

Mystery–Sex. Zoe Kohler, nondescript and mousy, dresses up from time to time and kills men she picks up in hotel bars. Retired captain Edward X. Delaney attempts to track down the "Hotel Ripper" killer.

Zoe has problems with sex, and Sanders has problems with the women's movement. Is it possible that the third deadly sin is envy?

The Case of Lucy Bending　　　　　　　　　　　　　PUTNAM, 1982

Drama–Sex. The story of a little girl who becomes a nymphomaniac and the community of greed and sexual abandon in which she lives. The central character is a child psychiatrist who finds he must understand the town, a typical Peyton Place, to help the child.

The Seduction of Peter S.　　　　　　　　　　　　　PUTNAM, 1983

Drama–Sex. Peter Scuro, unsuccessful actor, turns prostitute and then begins to recruit his friends in what becomes a major financial success. But the path to perdition opens swiftly. As payoffs grow to extortion, murder, and a tie-in with organized crime, Peter finds that he is caught in his own illusion.

SANTMYER, HELEN HOOVEN

Born in Ohio, 1895; educated at Wellesley College. She worked as an English professor, dean of women, and librarian. She began " . . . *And Ladies of the Club"* at the age of 38, as a rebuttal to Sinclair Lewis's satire *Main Street,* to show the virtues of small-town American life. She has also written *Herbs and Apples* (first published in 1925) and *The Fierce Dispute.* She died in 1986 at the age of 90.

" . . . And Ladies of the Club"   PUTNAM, 1984

Historical Novel–Saga. Some well-brought-up ladies in 1868 establish the literary Waynesboro (Ohio) Women's Club. Through the personal and political changes of the next 64 years, the club remains a point of continuity. The novel chronicles the lives, prejudices, and loyalties of its founding members and their descendants and gives a picture of small-town life at the time. The story and the lives of the last charter members end in 1932 with the coming of the New Deal.

SEGAL, ERICH

Born in Brooklyn, 1937; educated at Harvard. He has taught classics and comparative literature at Yale. In addition to writing scholarly books, he was coauthor of the screenplay for the Beatles' *Yellow Submarine* and wrote the screenplays for his novels *Love Story* and *Oliver's Story.* He was also a television commentator for the Olympic Games of 1972, 1976, and 1980.

Love Story   HARPER & ROW, 1970

Drama. Oliver Barrett IV, sports hero of Harvard, falls in love with poor Radcliffe music student Jenny Cavilleri. This short (125 pp.) novel traces the first years of their marriage and Oliver's difficult relationship with his father until the time that Jenny is found to be terminally ill with leukemia. The novel was fleshed out from a screenplay and then turned back into a movie.

Oliver's Story   HARPER & ROW, 1977

Drama. A sequel to *Love Story.* Two years after Jenny's death, Oliver is still unable to come to terms with his grief or deal with his father. He consults a psychiatrist, dates the beautiful president of a chain of department stores, and travels to Hong Kong along his way to self-discovery.

SERLING, ROBERT

Born in New York State, 1918; educated at Antioch College. He served in the army from 1942 to 1944 as an instructor in aircraft identification. He received numerous awards for aviation news reporting. Serling has been a United Press reporter and an editor for aviation journals. He has written fiction and nonfiction on flying, including the novels *The Left Seat; She'll Never Get off the Ground;* and *Wings.*

The President's Plane Is Missing   DOUBLEDAY, 1967

American Politics. Fatigued from the rigors of office, President Jeremy Haines announces plans for a short vacation. But en route to Palm Springs, Air Force One suddenly disappears. What follows is the detail of the workings of the press and the White House under the uncertainty of whether the president is alive or dead. Meanwhile, Vice-president Madigan, drenched in mediocrity, is on the verge of starting World War III.

SETON, ANYA

Born in New York City, 1916, the daughter of the author and naturalist Ernest Thompson Seton. She was educated with private tutors. She has written short stories and novels for more than 30 years, from *My Theodosia* in 1941 to *Smouldering Fires* in 1975. Her long-time interest in reincarnation and the occult is reflected in *Green Darkness*.

Green Darkness   HOUGHTON MIFFLIN, 1972

Historical Novel. When Celia marries into an aristocratic family, she begins to be haunted by strange memories and terrors. What do they mean, and why is her new husband so angry with her? As Celia hovers near death in a trance, a kindly Indian mystic seeks to help, taking Celia back 400 years to a girl who was buried alive, a romance with a priest, family intrigue, and the religious wars of 16th-century England.

SEUSS, DR. (PSEUDONYM OF THEODORE SEUSS GEISEL)

Born in Massachusetts, 1904; educated at Dartmouth, Lincoln, and Oxford University in England. He is a humorist, illustrator, and producer of films, and has won numerous awards for his work, including Emmy and Academy Awards. He is the president, publisher, and editor in chief of Beginner Books, Inc., a division of Random House. Seuss is best known for his stories for children, but has recently published two books for adults, *You're Only Old Once* and *The Seven Lady Godivas*.

The Butter Battle Book   RANDOM HOUSE, 1984

Juvenile–War. A parable in poetry on the insanity of war and the arms race. The battle is between the Yooks, who eat their bread with the butter side up, and the Zooks, who keep the butter side down. Both go to war, have brain trusts, and develop better weapons and counterweapons. The book ends with a Yook and a Zook each holding a bomb ready to go at the other.

SHAW, IRWIN

Born in New York City, 1913; educated at Brooklyn College. His short stories first appeared in the *New Yorker* in the 1930s. He published novels for almost 40 years, from the 1940s until the 1980s: his first was *The Young Lions* and his last *Acceptable Losses*. He has also written plays and films. He died in Switzerland in 1984.

Rich Man, Poor Man   DELACORTE, 1970

Saga. The story of Rudolph, Gretchen, and Thomas Jordache, children of a bitter German immigrant. Although two leave home in disgrace and the other finds wealth and prestige, they all are pursuing the American Dream of happiness. Shaw gives an unsentimental view of society from the end of World War II to the late 1960s as he shows the failures of his characters and the difference that money can make.

In the Preface to *Beggarman, Thief*, Shaw says that any resemblance between his book *Rich Man, Poor Man* and the film version of the story is purely coincidental.

Evening in Byzantium   DELACORTE, 1973

Glamour–Drama. Jesse Craig, a famous film producer, is severely disillusioned with his life and work. Prompted by a young reporter's questioning at the Cannes Film Festival, he takes a new look at his past and present and takes steps to save his life.

Beggarman, Thief   DELACORTE, 1977

Saga. The next generation of characters from *Rich Man, Poor Man* is portrayed. Billy gets involved with international terrorists, Gretchen makes a movie, and Wesley sets out to avenge his father's death. No one in the story is a beggarman or a thief.

The Top of the Hill   DELACORTE, 1979

Drama–Sex. A man brought up by an overprotective mother takes to a life of danger and physical testing. The story tells of his various adventures—skydiving, skiing, and the many women he has affairs with—and how he gets the chance to rescue a dying man from another overprotective woman.

SHELDON, SIDNEY

Born in Chicago, 1917; he attended Northwestern University for one year, and served in the air force in 1941. A novelist, playwright, and screen writer, Sheldon has written scripts for eight Broadway plays, more than 30 movies, and some 250 television shows. His first novel, *The Naked Face*, was nominated for an Edgar Award by the Mystery Writers of America. He received an Oscar for Best Screenplay for *The Bachelor and The Bobby Soxer*, and a Tony for *Redhead*. He was the creator of "The Patty Duke Show" and "I Dream of Jeanie."

A Stranger in the Mirror   MORROW, 1976

Glamour–Sex. A Hollywood comedian and a would-be actress ride a roller coaster of fame and fortune—from nothing to everything and back to nothing again. Blackmail, vengeance, pornographic films, true romance, medical nightmares, and miraculous recoveries are all part of the action.

Bloodline   MORROW, 1978

Suspense. When her father is killed, Elizabeth Roffe inherits control of a giant pharmaceutical company. But someone wants to sabotage the company and is trying to kill her. At least one of the joint stockholders is a murderer already, and another is probably insane. There is Ivo, who needs $1 million in a hurry; Hélène, the sadistic racing-car driver; and the ambitious Rhyss Williams, whom Elizabeth would like to marry.

Rage of Angels   MORROW, 1980

Drama–Sex. Attorney Jennifer Parker is attractive, brilliant, and determined to succeed. But she must make choices between love and principle and decide what her relationship will be with a United States senator and a Mafia boss. Soon crime and betrayal bring a chain of events that Jennifer cannot control, and her life, career, and son are threatened.

Master of the Game   MORROW, 1982

Drama–Sex. On her 90th birthday, Kate Blackwell looks back on a life of violence and ambition. She has succeeded in business and become rich and powerful, but her efforts to found a dynasty have been less successful. In fact, the family fortunes include murder, sadism, deliberate disfigurement, a son driven to insanity, and a five-year-old who tried to kill her sister. Kate has won at some games but lost at others.

If Tomorrow Comes   MORROW, 1985

Drama. Young Tracy Whitney is framed for a crime she did not commit. So begins a series of adventures in which Tracy gets revenge and enters into a rivalry with fellow con artist Jeff Stevens. From stealing art treasures to faking master-class chess, Tracy must use her wits to escape detection and gain romance and fortune.

SMITH, MARTIN CRUZ

Born in Pennsylvania, 1942; educated at the University of Pennsylvania. He wrote for the Associated Press and the magazine *For Men Only*. His novels include *Nightwing*, nominated for an Edgar Award, *The Analog Bullet*, and *Stallion Gate* (1987). Smith has written under his real name and such pen names as Jake Logan, Martin Quinn, Simon Quinn, and Nick Carter.

Gorky Park   RANDOM HOUSE, 1981

Mystery. Russian homicide inspector Arkady Renko finds three frozen bodies, mutilated beyond recognition, under the snow in Gorky Park. As the investigation goes on and bodies, or at least parts of them, continue to turn up, Renko realizes that the KGB does not want the matter solved. He proceeds nevertheless, and puts his own career and life in jeopardy.

SOLOMON, RUTH

Born in Kiev, Russia, 1908; educated at Syracuse University with graduate work at the University of Vienna. She is also the author of *The Ultimate Triumph* (1974) and *The Wolf and the Leopard* (1976).

The Candlesticks and the Cross   PUTNAM, 1967

Historical Novel–Saga. In turn-of-the-century Russia, the noble von Glasman family is caught up in the political conflicts and upheaval of the time. Tatars threaten the Ukraine, the Jews begin to be persecuted, and the mad monk Rasputin rules the court. Ronya von Glasman, with her fierce Tatar husband, undertakes a heroic fight for freedom. This is an autobiographical account of the author's own family. She still has the ring that young Rachel wears at the end of the novel.

SOLZHENITSYN, ALEXANDER ISAYEVICH

Born in Russia, 1918; educated at the University of Rostov-on-Don, where he studied math and physics. He joined the Red Army in 1941, and in 1945 was arrested for making critical remarks about Stalin. He spent eight years in a labor camp and three years in exile. *Cancer Ward* appeared in 1968. Although he won the Nobel Prize for Literature in 1970, he was not allowed to leave Russia to accept it. After writing *The Gulag Archipelago*, he was deported and settled in the United States.

The First Circle HARPER & ROW, 1968

Drama. An account of life in Russia during the time of Stalin. Mavrino is a scientific institute staffed with prisoners who are fed well and allowed to do their own work; nevertheless, they are in prison. Like the ancient philosophers in Dante's first circle, these people are in hell. Through a series of portraits we are shown the humanity and spirit of the prisoners; but the author also shows, with sharp irony, the terror and oppression throughout Russia at the time. Translated from the Russian by Thomas Whitney.

August 1914 FARRAR, STRAUS & GIROUX, 1972

War. The novel presents the reasons for Russia's defeat by the Germans in the Battle of Tannenberg in World War I. Showing extensive research and an understanding of military science, the battle scenes are set forth with precision. The action focuses on the historical figure General Samsonov and the fictional Colonel Vorotyntsev, who witnesses the disaster and attempts to see that the truth is made known. Translated from the Russian by Michael Glenny.

The Russian text was first published in Paris in 1971. A 1986 version of the book has been revised and enlarged to twice the original length, as the author promised.

SOUTHERN, TERRY, AND MASON HOFFENBERG

Southern: Born in Texas, 1926; educated at Southern Methodist University and the University of Chicago. He is known primarily as a writer of satirical screenplays, such as *Dr. Strangelove; Barbarella; Easy Rider;* and *The Cincinnati Kid.* He has also written the novel *The Magic Christian,* which, like *Candy,* is a satire. Southern says, "The world has no grounds for complacency. . . . Where you find smugness you find something worth blasting. I want to blast it" (*Contemporary Authors New Revision Series,* I: 618). Hoffenberg: Born in 1922. He wrote novels under several pen names for Olympia Press in Paris, where *Candy* was originally published. He died in 1986.

Candy   PUTNAM, 1964
Sex. Satire mixed with slapstick. This short book recounts the adventures of the lovable Candy with her father, uncle, professor, several
doctors, a hunchback, and a Zen teacher.

First published in Paris in 1958, the book was banned by the French
government as indecent. A shorter, edited version appeared in England.

STEEL, DANIELLE
Born in New York City, 1948(?); educated in France. She has worked
in public relations and advertising and is the mother of nine children
from three marriages. Her many novels include *Kaleidoscope; Once in a
Lifetime;* and *A Perfect Stranger.* In an exclusive *Family Circle* interview
(May 17, 1988), she explains how she combines babies and best sellers.
Recently she has produced one baby and one best seller a year.

Remembrance   DELACORTE, 1981
Saga. Serena, once an Italian princess and then an orphan and war
refugee, falls in love with a handsome American major. She finds love
and hatred, great success, and a violent death. Then the life of her
daughter is recounted.

Changes   DELACORTE, 1983
Glamour. Melanie Adams is a famous television newscaster in New York
when she meets Peter Hallam, a famous heart surgeon in Los Angeles.
She has two children, and he has three. How Melanie faces the long-
distance romance, her choice between career and marriage, and the
various crises with the children is the subject of this story.

Full Circle   DELACORTE, 1984
Drama. Tana Roberts is a lawyer whose career is easier than her romances. After relationships with several men, Tana must decide at age
39 if she will marry and have children.

Family Album   DELACORTE, 1985
Drama–Glamour. The story of Faye and Ward Thayer and their five
children over 40 years—from their success in Hollywood to their poverty, then back to their success as director and producer. Meanwhile,
their children grow up, and their lives are affected by such things as
homosexuality, drugs, jealousy, and the Vietnam War.

STEGNER, WALLACE
Born in Iowa, 1909; educated at the University of Utah, then became
a professor at Stanford. The author of many novels, his *Angle of Repose*
won a Pulitzer Prize, and *The Spectator Bird* won a National Book Award.
Other novels include *The Big Rock Candy Mountain; Fire and Ice; On a
Darkling Plain;* and *Crossing to Safety.* He has also written short stories
and some nonfiction, dealing especially with the West and nature.

All the Little Live Things   VIKING, 1967
Drama. A memoir of a young woman told by Joe Allston, a retired
literary agent living with his wife in northern California in the 1960s.

The woman had meant a great deal to the Allstons, particularly Joe. She respected all forms of life, brought people together, and taught them how to live. Yet she was dying of cancer all the while.

STEWART, FRED MUSTARD

Born in Indiana, 1936; educated at Lawrenceville and Princeton, and received a degree in history. He also served in the Coast Guard. Other books he has written are *The Mephisto Waltz; Six Weeks;* and *A Rage against Heaven.*

Century   MORROW, 1981

Historical Novel–Saga. The story of the building and preservation of a dynasty, spanning four generations to end in 1960. It begins in Sicily with two brothers, Franco and Victor. Franco is sent to prison by the jealous husband of Princess Sylvia dell'Acqua, while the younger Victor is sent to America to be adopted by one of the princess's friends. The story shows their struggles as they fight for freedom, success, and love. But when the dynasty is threatened by shame, it is Victor's granddaughter who must save it.

STEWART, MARY

Born in Sunderland, England, 1916; educated at Durham University, where she later taught English language and literature. She was married in 1945 to Sir Frederick Stewart, a Fellow of the Royal Society. Her first novel was *Madam, Will You Talk?* (1954), and since then she has written numerous books, including her Merlin trilogy, an account of the Arthurian legend. She also writes books for young readers.

This Rough Magic   MORROW, 1964

Suspense. The classical setting of the Greek island of Corfu excites a young actress from England who is visiting her sister. Soon she realizes that the people she meets all seem to be hiding things about themselves. Before her vacation is over, she will befriend a dolphin, find romance, and nearly get killed.

Airs above the Ground   MORROW, 1965

Suspense. Young Mrs. March sees her husband in a newsreel of a circus fire in Austria, but he is supposed to be on business in Stockholm. So when she is asked to escort a 17-year-old boy to Vienna to meet his father, she jumps at the chance. When the two arrive and find the circus, they become involved in intrigue and danger, and soon find out her husband's secret.

The Gabriel Hounds   MORROW, 1967

Suspense. While touring the Middle East, Christy encounters her cousin Charles, who is there on business. They both are curious to visit their great-aunt Harriet, who is living eccentrically in Lebanon, but getting into her "palace" is another matter. Christy feels that something is wrong at Harriet's home, and there is something that Charles will not tell her.

Soon the two are faced with great danger as they are kidnapped and learn the terrible truth.

The Crystal Cave   MORROW, 1970
Historical Novel–Adventure. The first in her series of books about the legend of King Arthur and Merlin. The story traces Merlin's life from boyhood to maturity. Here the secret of his parentage is explained, and so is the mystery of his powers. As he grows up, he serves different kings in his quest for the one who will unite all of Britain. And so the story ends with Merlin's fundamental role in the conception of the child who will one day be King Arthur. Stewart adds her own twists to the typical Arthurian legend.

The Hollow Hills   MORROW, 1973
Historical Novel–Adventure. The Arthurian legend continues. This is the story of Arthur's birth and childhood to the point when he becomes king, although barely a young man. Whereas the complications of Merlin's parentage were shown in *The Crystal Cave*, here Arthur's parentage is discussed and questioned. It is Merlin who takes him as a baby and teaches him, hiding the truth that he is King Uther's son until he can prove himself with the sword in the stone.

The Last Enchantment   MORROW, 1979
Historical Novel–Adventure. The third book in the series. The early years of Arthur's reign are recounted from Merlin's point of view. Arthur's son Modred is born, Camelot is built, and Arthur establishes his kingdom. He falls in love with Guinevere, although Merlin warns him not to. The magician himself has a romance, but his powers and very life may be jeopardized.

The Wicked Day   MORROW, 1983
Historical Novel–Adventure. The conclusion to the Arthurian legend. Merlin is no longer at the center of the action. The focus of this book is on Modred, Arthur's son. The boy has been raised by a fisherman and has no idea of his parentage until an incident reveals it to him. He is taken to Camelot, where a unique bond develops between him and Arthur. But jealousies arise, and tensions build to a wicked climax.

STONE, IRVING

Born in California, 1903; educated at the University of California and the University of Southern California. In addition to many biographical novels, Stone has written conventional biography as well, including books on Jack London, Earl Warren, and Clarence Darrow.

Those Who Love   DOUBLEDAY, 1965
Historical Novel. An account of Abigail and John Adams told from Abigail's point of view, from her first meeting with John to the close of his presidency in 1801. The book is crowded with events and details, as Stone tries to give the history of the man, in his rise from lawyer to diplomat to president, and a history of the new nation. Through all the years, the Adamses' marriage remains a source of strength.

The Passions of the Mind DOUBLEDAY, 1971
Historical Novel. A fictional biography of Sigmund Freud, from his early studies to his break with traditional medicine and the slow but shattering discovery of the world of the unconscious. The book also gives a picture of psychology in its early years and the culture and fashions of Vienna at the time.

The Greek Treasure DOUBLEDAY, 1975
Historical Novel. The story of the 19th-century archaeologist Henry Schliemann and his wife, Sophie, who discover the ruins of Mycenae and the site of Homer's Troy. There is little action in this story, however, as the couple perseveres through the difficulties of the first years of marriage, the disbelief of academics, and the obstacles created by the Greek government.

The Origin DOUBLEDAY, 1980
Historical Novel. An account of Charles Darwin from the time he was a young man in search of a profession to his work on evolution and natural selection. Stone draws on five years of research and an extensive bibliography for this detailed portrait of the naturalist: including his journey on the *Beagle*, domestic life and friendships, and the storm of controversy that his works provoked.

The book has received more praise than some of Stone's other novels. Historian A. L. Rowse, for example, called it "an extraordinary achievement" in providing a glimpse of the man Darwin behind the world-famous name.

STRAUB, PETER
Born in Wisconsin, 1943; educated at the University of Wisconsin-Madison and Columbia. He worked as a schoolteacher and experimented with various kinds of writing, including poetry, but it was the horror story that brought him commercial success. He is the author of *If You Could See Me Now* and *Shadowland* and the coauthor of *The Talisman* (see Stephen King).

Ghost Story COWARD, MCCANN, & GEOGHEGAN, 1979
Horror. The structure of the book gives us stories within a story, and action that moves backward over time. The elderly members of the Chowder Society tell tales of the strange and supernatural, but one by one they are succumbing to terrible deaths. Why do they look as if they had been scared to death? And what does this have to do with an event that happened 50 years before?

STYRON, WILLIAM
Born in Virginia, 1925; educated at Duke University, and served in the Marine Corps. *Lie Down in Darkness* (1951) was his first novel. He has also written *Set This House on Fire* and *The Long March*, the story of a forced march in a Marine training camp.

The Confessions of Nat Turner
RANDOM HOUSE, 1967

Historical Novel. Nat Turner, leader of the slave uprising in Southampton, Virginia, in 1831, tells his own story. The book begins after Nat has been apprehended and the uprising has been quelled, and then turns back to his experiences as a slave from childhood. We are shown Nat's psychological torment, his attitudes toward the black and white people he knows, and his complex emotions about violence, pity, and God.

Styron based the book on an actual historical event, including a 20-page pamphlet entitled "The Confessions of Nat Turner." The few facts that are known about the uprising are included in the story; the rest Styron calls "a meditation on history."

Sophie's Choice
RANDOM HOUSE, 1979

Drama–War. In 1947 a young southerner, Stingo, comes to a Brooklyn rooming house and meets a strange couple: the beautiful Sophie, Gentile and survivor of Auschwitz; and Nathan, Jewish, who fluctuates between great humor and dark rages. Infatuated by Sophie, Stingo begins to get pieces of her story, out of chronological order and also mixed with lies. The suspense builds as Sophie's story begins to come out.

SUSANN, JACQUELINE

Born in Philadelphia, 1918. She appeared in plays on Broadway and on television. She was married to movie producer Irving Mansfield for almost 30 years, and died of cancer in 1974.

Valley of the Dolls
BERNARD GEIS, 1966

Glamour–Sex. The story follows the lives of three women through romances, show-business success, and finally to drugs in the Valley of the Dolls. The Valley is Hollywood, and the Dolls are pills.

While Susann's draft was heavily edited by the publisher, much of the success of the book can be attributed to her own promotion efforts, according to biographer Barbara Seaman (*Lovely Me*). As of the late 1980s, this was the top-selling novel.

The Love Machine
SIMON & SCHUSTER, 1969

Glamour–Sex. Robin Stone can feel no emotion; yet women love him and chase him. As he rises to the top of the network's news division, he has affairs with a beautiful fashion model and a beautiful journalist, among others. Along the way he learns the secret of his past, and finally, he is able to tell one woman he needs her. Robin is not alone, though, in his inability to love. In this tale of Beautiful People and network politics, most of the liaisons, and the marriages too, are as cold as he is.

Once Is Not Enough
MORROW, 1973

Glamour–Sex. The story of an oppressive love between film star Mike Wayne and daughter January. They marry others and have affairs with glamorous people like themselves, but their overly close relationship blights January's life. Theirs is not the only unusual relationship in the story. Mike's wife, Dee, has a young cousin, David, who may marry January although he is in love with 53-year-old Karla, who is also loved by Dee.

Dolores MORROW, 1976

Glamour–Sex. Dolores is the young widow of an assassinated president. Now alone and too poor to sustain her standards of spending, she sets out to find money and a man. There is no real resemblance to any living person in this brief sketch.

SUTTON, HENRY (PSEUDONYM OF DAVID SLAVITT)

Born in White Plains, New York, 1935; educated at Yale, with a master's degree from Columbia. Slavitt has been a poet, playwright, novelist, and critic. He resigned in 1965 as film critic for *Newsweek* to begin writing full-time at Cape Cod. Best known for his poetry, he has also written serious novels (*Feel Free* and *Day Sailing*), as well as the more sensational, such as *The Voyeur*; *The Exhibitionist*; and *Vector*.

The Exhibitionist BERNARD GEIS, 1967

Glamour–Sex. Meredith and Merry Houseman are father and daughter, and both are film stars. Merry grows up in an atmosphere dominated by her father's many affairs. As she searches for the happiness denied her, she begins a series of affairs of her own.

TARR, HERBERT

Born in New York, 1929; educated at Brooklyn College, Columbia University, and the Hebrew Union College; ordained as a rabbi. Tarr wrote one earlier novel, *The Conversion of Chaplain Cohen*, while he was an air force chaplain in Labrador. His novels are strongly autobiographical.

Heaven Help Us! RANDOM HOUSE, 1968

Religion. Account of a rabbi who tries to bring religion to his suburban congregation. His parishioners, however, are more concerned with the social life, the temple fashion shows, and the tone of the Bar Mitzvahs. Some of the character sketches are biting, and the novel's humor has some sharp satiric edges.

THOMPSON, THOMAS

Born in Texas, 1933; educated at the University of Texas. He worked as a journalist for 12 years, becoming a staff writer for *Life* and Paris bureau chief. When *Life* ceased publication in 1972, he turned full-time to writing. *Blood and Money*, based on a real event, won the Edgar Allan Poe Award from the Mystery Writers of America. He also wrote the novel *Serpentine* and the script for the television movie *Callie and Son*. He died in 1982.

Celebrity DOUBLEDAY, 1982

Drama–Glamour. The future looks bright for three boys on the brink of high-school graduation. Kleber has talent, Mac has looks, and TJ has charm. Then a violent event occurs that will follow them on their very different paths to success and bring a new kind of publicity 25 years later.

Thompson commented, "Over the years at *Life* I'd written about many celebrities, and I wanted to write a novel exploring why anyone would *want to* be famous." (*Contemporary Authors New Revision Series*, 14:477).

THORP, RODERICK

Born in New York City, 1936; educated at City College of New York. His novel *The Detective* was made into a movie starring Frank Sinatra and released in 1968. Other novels include *Into the Forest*; *Dionysus*; and the recently published *Rainbow Drive*.

The Detective   DIAL, 1966

Mystery. A private detective is hired by a young widow to see if her husband's death was suicide or murder. The investigation, however, begins to connect with his own past and personal life; to solve the case, the detective must put his reputation and marriage on the line.

TOLKIEN, J. R. R. (JOHN RONALD REUEL)

Born in England, 1892; served with the Lancashire Fusiliers from 1915 to 1918. He was a professor of English language and literature at Oxford. In addition to many critical studies, he wrote *The Hobbit* (1937) and the *Lord of the Rings* trilogy (1954–55). He died in 1973. Over the course of his life, Tolkien developed a complete mythology and history of Middle Earth in the form of notes, tales, and lists of genealogy. These unfinished writings are now being edited and published by his son Christopher, also a teacher at Oxford.

The Silmarillion   HOUGHTON MIFFLIN, 1977

Science Fiction–Short Stories. A collection of tales and legends giving an account of the First Age of the World, to which the characters in *The Lord of the Rings* look back. Here is recorded the rebellion of Feanör and the other Elves, their exile and return to Middle Earth, and war against the Enemy. The three silmarils are jewels, created by Feanör, that alone hold the light of Valinor.

Published posthumously, as prepared and edited by Christopher Tolkien. A large glossary is included to help with the names and lineage.

Unfinished Tales   HOUGHTON MIFFLIN, 1980

Science Fiction–Short Stories. A collection of narratives, notes, and indexes relating to Tolkien's tales of Numenor and Middle Earth. A large part of the book consists of narrative fragments of the lives of some Tolkien characters. It is divided into four parts, representing the three Ages of the World and a short appendage.

Edited with commentary and indexes by Christopher Tolkien. Published posthumously. Like *The Silmarillion*, these tales are for the serious devotee of the history of Middle Earth and not for all *Lord of the Rings* readers.

TREVANIAN (PSEUDONYM OF RODNEY WHITAKER)

Born in Tokyo, 1925. He was formerly a professor of film and drama at the University of Texas, Austin, and is the author of *The Eiger Sanction*; *The Loo Sanction*; and *The Main*. Long unwilling to make his identity known, he says he writes under five different names on various subjects including theology, aesthetics, and film. (*Contemporary Literary Criticism* 29:429 includes his name—along with a picture, courtesy of the University of Texas News Service.)

Shibumi CROWN, 1979

Spy. Nicholai Hel has a Russian mother and a foster father who is a Japanese warrior. He speaks five languages and is adept at the game of Go. Through his experiences in war and prison, he has become the perfect assassin, "fighting terrorism" as he takes on the jobs he wants, but refusing governments he feels are unjust. The book traces his peculiar training and outlook on the world, and matches him against the Mother Company, a powerful secret international network which can even control the CIA.

The Summer of Katya CROWN, 1983

Historical Novel. It is the last summer before the guns of August 1914 and World War I. Jean-Marc Montjean, an innocent and somewhat obtuse young man, recently graduated from medical school, comes to a Basque village to be an assistant physician. There he meets Katya, her twin brother, and her father, and falls in love. But there is mystery to this family, with hints of violence and insanity, and soon the warmth and camaraderie of a festival are shattered by murder.

TRYON, THOMAS

Born in Hartford, 1926; he studied at Yale and the Art Students League, and served in the navy. In addition to writing best-selling novels, he has been an actor in film and stage productions, including *Richard III* and *Cyrano de Bergerac*. His latest novel is *All That Glitters*.

The Other KNOPF, 1971

Horror. The story of twin brothers Niles and Holland Perry—one is good and one is evil, and one is dead. But who is who? Eerie suspense and violence with good psychological characterization.

Harvest Home KNOPF, 1973

Horror. Ned and Beth Constantine have found their house in the country in an idyllic New England town. There is a Harvest Festival, a widow who heals with herbs, and even a village mystery. But an atmosphere of horror builds and begins to close around them, leading to the final chilling truth at Harvest Home.

The film does not capture the lyrical description and mood that are so much a part of the book.

Lady KNOPF, 1974

Drama. The story of a boy growing up in a small town in the 1930s and the mysterious "Lady" who captures his heart and imagination. A change

of pace for Tryon, who keeps the atmosphere and character without
the horror.

Crowned Heads   KNOPF, 1976

Short Stories—Glamour. Character sketches of four famous film stars.
Fedora lets people stand in for her and play parts of her life; Lorna
does not understand herself or the destruction she causes; Bobbitt, child
star of the 1950s, must try to grow up; and Willie is an old man guarding
his past until it is violently shattered. Read the stories in order for the
full impact.

UHNAK, DOROTHY

Born in the Bronx, 1933; she attended City College of New York but
dropped out to become a policewoman. She was promoted three times
and awarded the Outstanding Police Duty Medal, the department's
highest honor. During her years of service, she earned a degree in
criminology from the John Jay College of Criminal Justice. She is the
author of *False Witness*; *The Investigation*; and *Victims*, and still lives in
New York.

Law and Order   SIMON & SCHUSTER, 1973

Saga—Drama. The story of three generations of cops—the grandfather,
Sergeant O'Mally, murdered in a scandal and given a hero's funeral;
son Brian, the incorruptible by-the-book cop; and grandson Patrick,
torn between family and justice for his best friend's murder. Readers
also get details of police procedure and the life of an Irish Catholic
family in New York.

UPDIKE, JOHN HOYER

Born in Pennsylvania, 1932; educated at Harvard, and spent a year in
England at the Ruskin School of Drawing and Fine Art in Oxford. He
was on the staff of the *New Yorker* from 1955 to 1957 and won numerous
book awards, including the 1982 Pulitzer Prize for Fiction for *Rabbit Is
Rich*. In addition to novels, he writes poems and short stories. Recent
books are *Roger's Version, S.* and a collection of short stories entitled
Trust Me.

Couples   KNOPF, 1968

Drama—Sex. A satire set in a stylish Massachusetts suburb in the 1960s.
Tired of their work and their marriages, four couples keep exchanging
partners. Some lines are crossed and things change a little, but not much.

Bech: A Book   KNOPF, 1970

Drama. Seven episodes in the life of Henry Bech, a distinguished American author, as he travels in Russia and Eastern Europe, teaches at a
girls' school, engages in several romantic adventures, and develops writer's block.

Rabbit Redux   KNOPF, 1971

Drama. Harry Angstrom, hero of Updike's original *Rabbit, Run*, is now
10 years older and a linotype operator. Things still are not going very

well, however. Against the background of the social turmoil of the 1960s, he tries to deal with his family, his wife's infidelity, and some new friends of his own.

A Month of Sundays　　　KNOPF, 1975

Religion–Sex. Reverend Thomas Marshfield, 41, considers his life, his faith, and the events that led him to take an enforced vacation. A highly original character, Marshfield is full of sexual energy and authentic religious passion. The two combine and get confused, spilling over into a verbal inventiveness that is sustained throughout the novel.

The Coup　　　KNOPF, 1978

Drama. Political satire of a black dictator named Elleloû, head of the African state of Kush, his four wives, his rule, and his fall from power. He hates all things American but is powerless to stop the American influence on his country.

Rabbit Is Rich　　　KNOPF, 1981

Drama. It is 10 years later, and Rabbit is now 46 and a member of the middle class. He heads a Toyota dealership, lives with his wife and mother-in-law, and still tries to cope with events that seem to conspire against him.

URIS, LEON

Born in Baltimore, 1924; served in the Marines in World War II. His first novel, *Battle Cry*, based on his war experience, was published in 1953. He has also written the novel *Exodus* and screenplays including *Gunfight at the OK Corral*.

Armageddon　　　DOUBLEDAY, 1964

War. Uris tells of the rebuilding of Germany after World War II. Both the Americans and the Russians occupy the area, and conflicts among the three countries are present. Sean O'Sullivan, an American captain in charge of the military government of a city, has his own personal conflicts too, as his hatred of the Germans is juxtaposed with his love for a German girl.

Topaz　　　MCGRAW, 1967

Spy. A high KGB official defects to the U.S. and asks to talk to the French diplomat André Devereaux. Some 150 pages later, he reveals the existence of Topaz, a Russian spy network operating within France. He also tells of Soviet missiles in Cuba. Devereaux, caught in the middle between France and the United States, must decide how to use this information during the days of the Cuban Missile Crisis.

QB VII　　　DOUBLEDAY, 1970

Drama. An autobiographical novel tracing the lives of two adversaries who will meet in a courtroom trial. One is plaintiff Sir Adam Kelno, a Polish Catholic doctor who is charged with conducting concentration-camp experiments for the Nazis, and who sues for libel. The other adversary is bestselling novelist Abraham Cady, who writes a book about the Holocaust. They confront each other—and British justice—in the courtroom called Queen's Bench Seven.

Exodus provoked a trial (*Dering* v. *Uris*) in 1964 in which a surviving camp doctor sued the novelist for libel. Dering technically "won" because Uris had overstated the number of operations he performed, but the court awarded the doctor only a half-penny, as an insult.

Trinity   DOUBLEDAY, 1976
Saga–Historical Novel. The story covers 75 years in the lives of three families living in the north of Ireland in the 19th century. Each family is representative of a different socioeconomic situation, and yet they are interrelated. One family consists of Catholic hill-farmers; another, of a dynasty of British aristocracy; and the third, of shipyard workers of Scottish Presbyterian descent.

The Haj   DOUBLEDAY, 1984
International Intrigue. The story of "Haj" Ibrahim, head man of a Palestinian village, as told by his son. In the course of the narrative, Uris gives a detailed (and very critical) picture of Arab life and culture, with its passionate hatreds and brutality. Interspersed with the story are the chief historical events from 1922 to 1956.

As many reviewers pointed out, Uris is as unsympathetic to the people in *Haj* as he is sympathetic in *Exodus* and *Trinity*.

VAN SLYKE, HELEN
Born in Washington, D.C., 1919. She was a newspaper and magazine editor, was president of a perfume and cosmetic company, and was well known in fashion circles. She wrote *The Rich and the Righteous*; *All Visitors Must Be Announced*; and *Always Is Not Forever*, among a total of nine novels. Her last book, *No Love Lost*, was completed a few days before she went into the hospital for a liver operation from which she never recovered. She died in 1979.

A Necessary Woman   DOUBLEDAY, 1979
Drama. A shipboard romance and marital intrigue lead to a tragedy and a time of decision for 38-year-old Mary Farr Morgan, who must choose between love and a career.

Especially for readers who believe that career women are "unfulfilled" and that homosexuality is "an affliction."

No Love Lost   LIPPINCOTT, 1980
Saga. In this relatively short book, Van Slyke tells the story of five marriages and more than a half-dozen affairs. Lindsay grows up in a home with an unhappy marriage and has troubles of her own with two husbands. Meanwhile, her childhood friend Adele is having difficulties with several members of Lindsay's family. Will Lindsay make her second marriage work, or will she return to her first husband, now unhappily married to someone else?

VIDAL, GORE

Born in West Point, New York, 1925. He served in the army in World War II and published his first novel, *Williwaw*, at the age of 21. In addition to his many novels, he has written both films and plays and has published collections of essays and short stories. His novel *Duluth* appeared in 1983, and *Empire* in 1987. He also wrote mystery stories in the 1950s under the name of Edgar Box. He comes naturally to his work as a historical novelist and critic of American politics. His grandfather, Thomas Gore, was a United States senator, and his father, Eugene Vidal, served in Franklin Roosevelt's administration. The author himself ran for public office twice: once for Congress as a Democrat in a strongly Republican district and once in a Democratic primary for senator.

Julian   LITTLE, BROWN, 1964

Historical Novel. A new look at Roman Emperor Julian the Apostate, known for his attempt to stamp out Christianity in the 4th century A.D. The story is told from his point of view, through his memoirs. Julian comes to the throne as a young man after the rest of his family has been slaughtered. He is a brilliant 30-year-old, a philosopher and military genius. He fights against the political and religious changes threatening Rome at the time and is killed in a military campaign at the age of 32.

Washington, D. C.   LITTLE, BROWN, 1967

American Politics. Political intrigue in the nation's capital during the years 1937–1952. Senator Burton Day is powerful and ambitious, but others—including his assistant Clay Overbury—have ambitions of their own. All of the main characters are intelligent and keenly aware of what goes on around them. As they interact with each other in the tight circle of Washington's social life, readers are given a first-hand view of the events and politics of the time.

Myra Breckinridge   LITTLE, BROWN, 1968

Sex. The story of a man who becomes a woman and then, through an accident, becomes a man again. Along the way Myra seduces Rusty Godowsky, as well as his girlfriend, Mary Ann, in the process exacting her own kind of revenge. The novel serves as a vehicle for Vidal's satire on America, Hollywood, and attitudes toward sex.

The book was reprinted in a 1986 Random House edition along with the sequel *Myron* (Random House, 1974) and a new introduction by the author.

Burr   RANDOM HOUSE, 1973

Historical Novel–American Politics. An account of Aaron Burr's life as he confides it to a young journalist: his duel with Hamilton, trial for treason, marriages, and conflicts with the founding fathers. Since it is told from Burr's point of view—with occasional comments by the journalist—Vidal is deliberately showing the good in Burr and the less-than-heroic side of the traditional American heroes. Watch the careful construction of the novel right down to the shocking but logical conclusion.

1876   RANDOM HOUSE, 1976

Historical Novel–American Politics. A well-known writer returns from Europe to renew his acquaintance with his own country, find a way to make a living, and chronicle the election of 1876. Looking through the somewhat cynical eyes of his narrator, Vidal brings to life a period of corruption, with scandals in the White House, the buying and selling of offices, and election fraud. He shows such historical figures as President Grant, Tilden, Garfield, William Cullen Bryant, and others, and gives an amazingly detailed picture of New York and Washington at the time—complete with its new "friction" matches, costly five-dollar dinners, and goats in Central Park. Note: Tilden actually won the popular vote in the 1876 election, but lost the electoral vote to Hayes.

Creation   RANDOM HOUSE, 1981

Historical Novel. Cyrus Spitama, ambassador, courtier, and friend to the Persian king Xerxes, recounts his adventurous life. He knew Confucius, Socrates, and Pericles, traveled to India and China, and could say what really happened in the Greek and Persian War. Vidal gives detail on politics, war, religion, affairs at court, early education, food, and fashion in the 5th century B.C. And again he turns the lens of history away from the traditional point of view. Westerners learn of the 5th century from the Greeks; so Vidal shows the same history from the Persian point of view.

Lincoln   RANDOM HOUSE, 1984

Historical Novel–American Politics. Lincoln is seen from the outside by members of his cabinet, his wife, and his young secretary and assistant John Hay. A quiet figure given to droll jokes and shrewd political bargaining, Lincoln is capable of errors and weakness as well as strength. He conducts the wartime presidency, works with a cabinet of strong political rivals, and insists that the union will be preserved. According to Vidal, the person does not appear to be great, but he does great things. Other historical figures, too, are shown in detail: Secretary of State William Seward; the ambitious Salmon Chase and his even more ambitious daughter Kate; and Mary, Lincoln's mentally unstable wife who cannot resist wild spending sprees.

VINGE, JOAN

Born in Baltimore, 1948; educated at San Diego State. She worked as a salvage archaeologist before becoming a full-time science-fiction writer. Her short stories have been published in a number of magazines and anthologies.

Return of the Jedi   RANDOM HOUSE, 1983

Science Fiction–Juvenile. In this sequel to *Star Wars* and *The Empire Strikes Back*, the evil Galactic Empire and Darth Vader are completing a new Death Star. Han Solo is held captive by Jabba the Hutt, while the friends—Luke, Leia, Chewbacca, R2-D2, and C-3PO—come together to rescue him. The rebels then plan the destruction of the Death Star, while Luke must carry out his own special mission. The book followed the movie and includes many photos from it.

VONNEGUT, KURT JR.

Born in Indianapolis, 1922; educated at Cornell and the University of Chicago; drafted into the infantry in World War II. His novels include *Player Piano*; *Cat's Cradle*; *Sirens of Titan*; and *Mother Night*. He also writes short stories, plays, and essays and has written for television and hosted "Life on the Mississippi." His latest book is *Galápagos*.

Slaughterhouse-Five; or, The Children's Crusade   DELACORTE, 1969

War–Science Fiction. Vonnegut writes about his experience in World War II, particularly the destruction of Dresden and its civilian population by American bombs. To do this, he imagines Billy Pilgrim, who saw the bombing as a prisoner of war and later becomes an optometrist in Ilium, New York. As Billy goes insane, he sees himself transported to the planet of the Tralfamadorians and kept as a creature in their zoo. Billy is capable of time travel, but his journeys keep returning him to Dresden. A powerful antiwar novel.

Breakfast of Champions; or, Goodbye Blue Monday!   DELACORTE, 1973

Drama. Kilgore Trout, the science-fiction writer Vonnegut has used in earlier books, meets up with Dwayne Hoover, a midwestern Pontiac dealer who is in the process of going insane. Along the way, Vonnegut satirizes sex, racism, and other features of American society. He appears in his own story to set his characters free on his 50th birthday. He also adds pictures—of a chicken, Kentucky Fried Chicken, an electric chair—so that readers who may be from a different planet will know what life on Earth was like.

Slapstick; or, Lonesome No More!   DELACORTE, 1976

Science Fiction. Wilbur Daffodil II Swain, former U.S. president and now king of Manhattan, reflects on his past life. He tells of his twin sister, Eliza, and how they were both considered idiots until they put their heads together and became one perfect genius. His sister is killed in an avalanche on Mars, and he runs for president on the "Lonesome No More" platform, which assigns everyone new middle names and gives them an extended family. The story's time is the future, when plagues have nearly wiped out the world. But Swain celebrates his 100th birthday, communicates with his sister, and can still laugh and say "Hi ho."

Jailbird   DELACORTE, 1979

Drama–American Politics. A satirical look at American society, and its inequalities, from the 1930s through the 1970s, as seen through the eyes of Walter Starbuck, ex–Harvard man, obscure member of the Nixon White House, and jailbird.

WALLACE, IRVING

Born Irving Wallechinsky in Chicago, 1916; educated at Williams and Berkeley. He is the writer of many screenplays, including *The West Point Story*; *Meet Me at the Fair*; and *The Burning Hills*. He also wrote the novels *The Sunday Gentleman* and *The Celestial Bed* (1987). He is not the only best-selling writer in the family, however. He coauthored, with his son David Wallechinsky and daughter Amy Wallace, the popular nonfiction book *The People's Almanac*. The three also wrote *The Book of Predictions*.

The Man   SIMON & SCHUSTER, 1964

American Politics. When the president and Speaker of the House are accidentally killed, Douglas Dilman becomes the first black president of the United States. There are many people close to him, however, who wish to manipulate him for their own purposes. Opposition to Dilman leads to an assassination attempt, race riots, and an impeachment trial. But Dilman, at first hesitant and uncertain of his role, faces his opponents with honor and courage.

Wallace includes historical background on succession and impeachment. The book was written before the 25th Amendment reformed some of the problems with succession.

The Plot   SIMON & SCHUSTER, 1967

International Intrigue–American Politics. An ex-president, a reporter, a call girl, and a State Department official all have seen their reputations damaged in the past and seek to repair them. Through chance meetings at a summit conference in Paris, they get together and discover a plot much larger than their personal problems.

The Seven Minutes   SIMON & SCHUSTER, 1969

Drama. A book becomes the center of a controversy and trial on the grounds of being pornographic. Attorney Mike Barrett, who defends the book, must discover who the author really is and find the woman on whose love affair the questionable passages are based.

Wallace captures the attitudes for and against censorship and includes background information on the issue.

The Word   SIMON & SCHUSTER, 1972

Religion. An archaelogical discovery has revealed a new text of the life of Jesus, promising the modern world a tremendous rebirth of faith. But the group of book publishers, clerics, and biblical scholars who will be bringing forth the new Bible have their own selfish motives bound up in the discovery. When young public-relations man Steven Randall is hired to publicize the event, he is plunged into intrigue and lied to at every turn. Is the material real or a forgery, and who is lying and who is telling the truth?

The Fan Club   SIMON & SCHUSTER, 1974

Drama–Glamour–Sex. Young writer Adam Malone has a fantasy about film goddess Sharon Fields. When he shares his dream with a salesman, an accountant, and a car mechanic, the fantasy becomes real, leading to kidnapping and rape. In order to escape, actress Fields must stage the best production of her career. At the same time, however, the men are changing, as reality makes the dream disappear.

The R Document   SIMON & SCHUSTER, 1976

American Politics. A proposed 35th Amendment to the Constitution would limit the freedoms protected by the Bill of Rights. The author of the amendment, and the secret R Document that will accompany it, is FBI director Vernon Tynan, who wants dictatorial power for himself. Young attorney general Christopher Collins must find the document and stop Tynan—but Tynan is out to stop him.

WAMBAUGH, JOSEPH

Born in 1937. The only child of an East Pittsburgh policeman and an upstairs maid, Wambaugh went to California at the age of 14. He served in the Marines, worked in a steel mill, and earned an English degree before joining the Los Angeles Police Department in 1960. He began writing at the age of 30, and his first novel, *The New Centurions*, earned him a reprimand for criticizing the department. Besides his police fiction, he also wrote the nonfiction books *The Onion Field* and *Echoes in the Darkness*. He wants to show the life and stress of being a police officer, and in a *Time* interview in 1981, he said, "You like to think that your work has some impact."

The New Centurions   LITTLE, BROWN, 1970

Drama. Story of three cops on the Los Angeles police force—their troubles, routines, street life, and camaraderie. The men are Serge Duran, ex-Marine and Chicano; Roy Fehler, a liberal intellectual; and Gus Plebesly, who has to find out about his courage and manhood. The book provides detail and atmosphere of the city and the crime around them.

The Blue Knight   LITTLE, BROWN, 1972

Drama. Bumper Morgan, 20-year veteran policeman, is sentimental, guilty of police brutality, somtimes comic, and in love with his badge and his job. The story tells of his last three days before retirement, his reminiscences about the past, and a decision.

The Choirboys   DELACORTE, 1975

Drama. The Choirboys are 10 cops on the night shift who get together in Los Angeles's MacArthur Park after work for "choir practice." The men are by turns rough, bawdy, funny, and pathetic. We see them at roll call, in a shootout with ducks, and through to the final tragedy in the park. The conflicts they face are mostly against their own cynicism and private terrors.

The Black Marble   DELACORTE, 1978

Mystery. Sargeant Valnikov is an excellent police officer and exiled Russian with a drinking problem and a 19-year-long nightmare. Philo Skinner is a dog handler-turned-extortionist who loves dogs but has trapped himself into killing them. These and other unique characters collide in a tale of police routine, dog shows, and a real love story.

The Glitter Dome   MORROW, 1981

Mystery–Sex–Glamour. Two Hollywood policemen investigate the
murder of a film studio head who may have been involved in child
pornography. Here the highjinks are more subdued, and the chill of
the private nightmares stronger than in other Wambaugh stories.

The Delta Star   MORROW, 1983

Mystery. Homicide detectives investigate the connection between the
murder of a hooker, Russian spies, and Caltech scientists. Meanwhile,
other assorted characters in the precinct engage in the violence and
craziness that Wambaugh readers have come to expect.

WELTY, EUDORA

Born in Mississippi, 1909; educated at Mississippi State College for
Women, the University of Wisconsin, and the Columbia Graduate
School of Business. She has published numerous short stories in the
Atlantic Monthly, the *New Yorker*, and other magazines. She is the recipient
of many honorary degrees and rewards for her writing. Other novels
include *The Robber Bridegroom* and *Delta Wedding*.

Losing Battles   RANDOM HOUSE, 1970

Drama. In the little town of Banner, Mississippi, in the 1930s, a family
gathers for the 90th birthday of Granny Vaughn. They eagerly await
the arrival of the oldest grandchild, Jack, who is supposed to be getting
out of the state penitentiary. The members of the family and the townspeople all have their battles to fight against a changing way of life. Welty
relates their stories through rich and extensive dialogue.

WEST, JESSAMYN

Born in Indiana, 1907; educated at Whittier College. She wrote novels,
short stories, poems, autobiographies, and travel diaries, which often
portrayed her own life of growing up on a farm. Novels include *The
Friendly Persuasion* (1945), *The Witch Diggers* (1951), and *A Matter of Time*
(1966); and her autobiographies are *Hide and Seek* (1973) and *The Woman
Said Yes* (1976). She died in 1984.

Except for Me and Thee   HARCOURT, 1969

Historical Novel. The day-to-day life of a Quaker couple at the time of
the Civil War is depicted. The Birdwells marry, move west, and become
involved in the Underground Railroad. West details their ordinary routines and the attempt to hold onto their own beliefs and customs.

Massacre at Fall Creek   HARCOURT, 1975

Historical Novel. In 1824 in Indiana, nine Seneca Indians were killed
by four white men and a boy. This is a fictionalized account of the
murders, the trial, and the verdict. West shows us the effect the incident
had on the families and the community, in what was apparently the first
time white men faced charges for killing Indians. The heroine of her
story is Hannah Cape: her father is a preacher, and her young brother

is a witness to the murders. Interwoven with the trial are her romances with some of the men involved.

WEST, MORRIS

Born in Melbourne, Australia, 1916. He served with the Australian army intelligence in World War II and then moved to Italy and began writing novels. He also worked as Vatican correspondent for the *Daily Mail*. His books include *The Devil's Advocate*; *The Shoes of the Fisherman*; and *Cassidy*.

The Ambassador   MORROW, 1965

Drama—War. A crisis point in the early American involvement in Vietnam as seen from the point of view of the American ambassador, a top professional but a deeply troubled man. Even as he begins to understand the situation and meet the people there, a question is building of the gravest political and moral importance. Only he can answer it.

An excellent account of the various sides of the Vietnam problem, written before most people were aware of them.

The Tower of Babel   MORROW, 1968

Spy—War. The story gives an in-depth view of several characters before the Six-Day War in the Middle East—an Israeli spy, a Syrian security chief, an individualist working for the PLO, and a shady international banker. As these men and their politics and religions clash, history is doomed to repeat itself.

The Salamander   MORROW, 1973

Spy. A general's death leads secret agent Dante Matucci on the trail of conspirators who wish to bring down the Italian republic. Soon his own director forces him off the case, and he must depend on the help of the mysterious and aristocratic Salamander. Matucci will face real evil and suffer great psychological torment before the case is closed.

Harlequin   MORROW, 1974

International Intrigue. The narrator and his friend George Harlequin are locked in a financial duel with a giant computer outfit and its head man, Basil Yanko. But Harlequin has his own magic to use in the rituals of international finance and terror. West adds comments on the power of magic and illusion.

Proteus   MORROW, 1979

International Intrigue. A president of a multinational firm uses his wealth and power to head Proteus, a secret group pledged to wipe out government tyranny and injustice. When his own family becomes the target of violence, he goes even further, challenging the nations of the world to make reforms or face destruction.

The Clowns of God   MORROW, 1981

Religion. In the last decade of the 20th century, Pope Jean Marie Barette has a vision that the end of the world is at hand. Forced to abdicate on grounds of insanity, he seeks the help of his friend, the scholar Mendelius, in persuading people about the truth of his vision. Although the book has little plot, it is divided into three sections. In Book I Mendelius faces the logical and moral questions raised by the vision; in Book II Jean Marie takes up his own cause; and in Book III a stranger helps.

WEST, REBECCA (PSEUDONYM OF CICELY ISABEL ANDREWS, NÉE FAIRFIELD)

Born in Ireland, 1892; educated at Edinburgh and at the Royal Academy of Dramatic Art in London. She began her journalistic career in 1911, writing for the feminist magazine *Freewoman*. She was a suffragette, a socialist, and a member of the Fabian Society. West wrote for the *New Statesman*, *Nation*, and *New Republic*, and published biographies and nonfiction as well as novels. She made a cameo appearance in the film *Reds* in 1981, and died in 1983. Her novel *Sunflower*, written during the 1920's, was published posthumously in 1987. Suppressed during her lifetime, it includes a fictionalized account of her relationship with H. G. Wells, by whom she bore a son.

The Birds Fall Down   VIKING, 1966

Drama–Spy. Europe on the eve of the Russian Revolution as seen through the eyes of Laura Rowan. Laura, a product of two cultures, is accompanying her grandfather, the count, on a train from Paris to Russia. They are confronted by a young revolutionary who tells the count that a trusted adviser is actually a double agent. Laura will learn more about treason, betrayal, and murder before her journey is over.

WHITE, TERENCE HANBURY

Born in India, 1906; educated at Cambridge. He taught school in England, resigning at the age of 30 to devote himself to writing. White is best known for his stories about the Arthurian legend. He wrote the children's books *The Sword in the Stone* and *Mistress Masham's Repose*. He died in 1964.

The Book of Merlyn   UNIVERSITY OF TEXAS PRESS, 1977

Historical Novel–War. The book opens with King Arthur, now an old man, on a battlefield. Merlyn comes to teach him one last lesson about war. With the help of magic and the power of the animal kingdom, Arthur is aided in his life's final decision.

White wrote this book in 1941 as the conclusion to *The Once and Future King*. Publication was delayed, however, because of the war and White's pacifism, and when *The Once and Future King* was finally published in 1958, this book did not appear with it. It was later discovered in the University of Texas archives and then published.

WHITNEY, PHYLLIS A.

Born in Yokohama, Japan, 1903. She began writing mysteries for young people before she wrote for adults, and won two Edgar Awards for her juvenile books. She has worked as a bookseller, librarian, and children's book editor, and has taught writing at New York University. Her book *Writing Juvenile Fiction* is a standard text in the field. Whitney was elected president of the Mystery Writers of America in 1975. She currently alternates between writing adult and juvenile novels, at a rate of about two a year. Some recent books are *Flaming Tree*; *Dream of Orchids*; and *Feather on the Moon*.

Columbella   DOUBLEDAY, 1966

Suspense. On St. Thomas, Jessica Abbott is asked by Maud Hampton to join her household and give guidance to Maud's granddaughter, Leila. But no one else wants her there, particularly Leila's mother, Catherine. Jessica must try to gain Leila's trust and break the terrible influence that her mother has over her. Some of the characters have secrets that Jessica soon stumbles onto, and she discovers why she is not welcomed.

Spindrift   DOUBLEDAY, 1975

Mystery. After being hospitalized because of her father's tragic death, Christy Moreland returns to her mother-in-law's estate to rebuild her life with her estranged husband and son. But, most important, she wants to discover why and how her father died. Her mother-in-law is determined to convince her that she is crazy, and someone else is warning her to leave. Will she be able to find someone there whom she can trust?

WICKER, TOM

Born in North Carolina, 1926; educated at the University of North Carolina. He has worked as a *New York Times* columnist and Washington bureau chief. Wicker wrote six novels between 1951 and 1961, and nonfiction also, then spent many years writing *Facing the Lions*. He is the author of the nonfiction books *Kennedy without Tears* and *A Time to Die*.

Facing the Lions   VIKING, 1973

American Politics. A story of conflict between ideals and ambition featuring Richmond Morgan, political reporter for a major East Coast newspaper, and his friend and presidential candidate Senator Hunt Anderson. On the occasion of Anderson's death, Morgan tries to find out what really happened the night his friend lost the nomination.

A rich source of authentic detail on political reporting and conventions.

WIESEL, ELIE

Born in Transylvania, 1928; educated at the Sorbonne, Paris. He moved to the United States in 1956, and was a professor of Judaic studies at City College of New York from 1972 to 1976. He is the author of many books on Judaic and biblical studies. Wiesel was the recipient of the 1986 Nobel Peace Prize.

A Beggar in Jerusalem   RANDOM HOUSE, 1970

Drama–Religion. At one level, the book tells the stories of characters who gather at the Wailing Wall in Jerusalem, and particularly of David, who looks for a friend supposedly killed in the Six-Day War. On another level, the characters become metaphors for larger statements about the Jewish experience and the human problem of killing and surviving.

WILDER, ROBERT

Born in Massachusetts, 1901; educated at Columbia. He was a newspaper reporter and columnist before he turned to writing fiction in the 1960s. Author of some 18 books and many screenplays, he lived in Florida and sailed and fished in the Bahamas. He died in 1974.

An Affair of Honor   PUTNAM, 1969

Drama. Max Hertog lives in the Bahamas and cares only for himself and the exercise of power. But Max's fortunes change when he begins to accumulate too many enemies, and soon intrigue and a black uprising lead to murder.

WILDER, THORNTON NIVEN

Born in Wisconsin, 1897; spent part of his childhood in China. He served in both World War I and II, achieving the rank of lieutenant colonel. He was educated at Yale, and became a professor of English at the University of Chicago. Like his character Theophilus North, Wilder was a man of many careers. Teacher, traveler, performer, soldier, and writer, he was the first to be awarded a National Medal for Literature. He is the author of the novels *The Cabala*; *The Woman of Andros*; and the Pulitzer Prize-winning *The Bridge of San Luis Rey*. He also won Pulitzer Prizes for his plays *Our Town* and *The Skin of Our Teeth*. He died in 1975.

The Eighth Day   HARPER & ROW, 1967

Saga–Historical Novel. The story of two families at the turn of the century in Coaltown, Illinois. John Ashley is accused of Breckenridge Lansing's murder and, when convicted, flees to Chile, leaving his family to face the hardships and hostility of the town. The story moves between the two families, back and forward through three generations. Life continues, says Wilder, past the seven days of creation into the eighth day.

Theophilus North   HARPER & ROW, 1973

Drama. Theophilus takes a tutoring job in Newport, Rhode Island. He finds that Newport is really nine separate cities, and that these cities correspond to the nine different careers he had wished to pursue. He goes through all of the cities and careers in the course of the novel, correcting various problems that he finds. Each chapter provides a new vignette on the life of the city in the 1920s.

Theophilus was the name of the author's twin brother, who died at birth.

WILLIAMS, KIT

Born in England, 1946(?). He worked in factories and electronics before starting work as an artist and writer in 1972. He wrote *Masquerade*, a puzzle contest, then *Masquerade: The Complete Book with Answers and Clues Explained*. He designed a different contest in 1984 in *Book without a Name*.

Masquerade SCHOCKEN, 1980

Mystery (puzzle contest). The Moon gives a jewel to Jack Hare to deliver to the Sun, but along the way he loses it. By the use of colorful pictures and clever riddles, Williams provides clues to figure out where the Hare lost the jewel.

The author really did create a jewel and hid it in England. The puzzle contest was solved.

WOUK, HERMAN (PRONOUNCED WOKE)

Born in New York City, 1915; graduated from Columbia University; served in the navy in World War II. He wrote jokes for radio comedians, including for the *Fred Allen Show*. He received a Pulitzer Prize for *The Caine Mutiny* and later adapted it into a play. He has written other plays and such well-known novels as *Marjorie Morningstar* and *Youngblood Hawke*. He has recently published the novel *Inside, Outside*.

Don't Stop the Carnival DOUBLEDAY, 1965

Drama. Norm Paperman, a struggling New York agent, decides to give it up and buy a hotel in the Caribbean. He is soon beset by a host of colorful characters and comic misadventures. He copes with earthquakes, scandals among the help, and a very unreliable partner, but then the calamities take a more serious turn.

The Winds of War LITTLE, BROWN, 1971

War–Saga. Commander Victor (Pug) Henry, USN, is assigned to Berlin as naval attaché in 1939, and so is on the scene as the winds of war move closer to the United States. His correct guess about the Nazi-Soviet Pact puts him in contact with President Roosevelt, whom he then serves as unofficial adviser. Historical events and documents are interwoven with details of Pug's personal life as his two sons go to war, his wife contemplates divorce, and he awaits his first battleship command.

War and Remembrance LITTLE, BROWN, 1978

War–Saga. A story of World War II from Pearl Harbor to Hiroshima as seen through the experiences of Captain Victor (Pug) Henry and his family and closest friends. Pug commands a ship in the Pacific, while one son is on a submarine and another takes part in the Battle of Midway. His Jewish daughter-in-law and her baby must attempt to escape the Holocaust while her uncle writes "A Jew's Journey" on his flight across Europe to Theresienstadt and Auschwitz.

As the author says in the Afterword, he attempts "to bring the past to vivid life through the experiences . . . of a few people caught in the war's maelstrom."

T   W   O

The Authors

Pᴇᴏᴘʟᴇ ᴡᴏɴᴅᴇʀ ᴡʜᴏ the author really is behind the famous name. Does she live as exciting a life as her heroine? Did he work at the job he is writing about? Knowing the answers to some of these questions can often increase the enjoyment of reading, although it can provide surprises and disappointments, too. So writers become celebrities. Book jackets tell "something about the author." Biographies are read avidly, often rivaling fictional books in popularity. Within the space of one year, Susann, Kazan, Buckley, Cheever, Roth, and Michael Crichton all had autobiographies or biographies published, following the books about Mailer, Michener, Jones, and Ambler which had recently appeared.

Background facts about the authors provide other information as well. They give a profile of the writers as a group so that they can be compared with other notable, and influential, figures. And they provide insight into the values and experience woven into the fiction. The age of the characters, their dreams and their nightmares, success and misfortunes—all will be viewed in a somewhat altered light. For all these reasons, this short chapter, like a book jacket, can help to introduce the chapters that follow. It provides facts about the authors, including dates and places of birth, education, and unique jobs and experience. It then makes some connections between the authors and the books, the fiction and the facts.

TABLE 1
Age

DECADE OF BIRTH					
Number of Authors[a]					
Before 1900	1900s	1910s	1920s	1930s	1940 and later
11	33	45	60	35	24

AGE OF AUTHORS WHEN THEIR FIRST BEST SELLERS WERE PUBLISHED[b]

Age	20s	30s	40s	50s	60s	70s	80s
Number	3	44	61	52	31	13	4

Median Age = 49

[a]Based on the 208 authors and coauthors for whom birth dates were available. Hoffman is not included.

[b]Their first best sellers *in the time period 1965–1985*. If an author published a book in 1963 and 1965, his age would be taken at 1965. Age was found by subtracting the author's birth date from publication date of the book.

Age

One is never too old, it seems, to write a best seller. Seventeen of the authors published their first at age 70 or older, and the average age for the *first* best seller among the books from 1965 to 1985 was a decidedly middle-aged 49. The youngest author was Michael Crichton at 27, and the oldest Helen Santmyer at 89.

There is no one typical age for these writers, as table 1 makes clear. Nevertheless, the largest number were born in the decade of the 1920s. Unlike the U.S. population as a whole, the authors are concentrated in middle age.[1] Only one representative of the 1950s makes the group—Douglas Adams, born in 1952. (E. T. A. Hoffman, born in 1776, is not included in the totals. His classic fairy tale *Nutcracker*, with illustrations by Maurice Sendak, became a best seller in 1984.)

Even if we look only at the authors of the 1980s, the average age does not decrease.[2] In fact, it increases slightly. The median and most frequent decade of birth for these authors was *still* the 1920s. Their median age at publication was 52. Mere youngsters such as Douglas Adams and Stephen King (b. 1947) were writing best sellers, but so were Irving Stone (1903), Helen Santmyer (1895), Louis L'Amour (1908), and Dr. Seuss (1904). L'Amour was writing books before Stephen King was born.

We have been able to find the year of birth for all but seven of the authors and coauthors. In cases where the birth date was followed by a question mark in the only available source, we have used that year. When all of the standard references omitted the year of birth, we assume the author did not care to have this information known.

The authors can be compared with another group of notables—United States senators. The senators, too, are predominantly middle-aged, averaging 50.5 years old in 1987. They won their first election to the Senate at the median age of 44. And like the authors, they often find that one success helps lead to another. They stay in the Senate as the authors stay on the best-selling lists. For another comparison, a "media elite" can be identified in American society, consisting of the top columnists, editors, and executives at the most influential news media outlets. These include the major national newspapers, weekly magazines, and television networks. This media elite, composed primarily of individuals in their thirties and forties, is substantially younger than the best-selling authors.[3]

To round out the statistics on age, 49 of the authors were dead as of the end of 1987. The male authors had lived to age 65, on the average, and the women authors to a venerable 78.[4]

Birthplace

In some places people grow up to be farmers, fishers, or major-league ball players. But does birthplace affect the odds of becoming a best-selling writer? Does it matter where one is born?

The answer, with one significant exception, appears to be not very much. Overall, the number of authors born in a particular place is proportionate to the population. The states largest in population have the most best-selling writers, but they have the most doctors, bricklayers, and salespeople, too. In other words, birthplace in the United States gives little special benefit or disadvantage: the North Dakota prodigy can aspire to fame and fortune just like her counterpart in Illinois. More than two-thirds of the states have produced at least one best-selling writer. Alaska, Florida, Vermont, and a few others are still waiting their turn.

The exception is New York. Although it is not four times larger in population than some other states, it claims more than four times the number of authors. About one-fourth of the 216 authors and coauthors came from that one state, with most of them, 42, from New York City. Illinois is a weak second with 14. It is not enough, apparently, to come to the publishing capital of the world to seek one's fortune—it helps to be born there.

The media elite is often charged with being too northeastern in outlook.[5] The authors could be subject to the same criticism. Of course, this still leaves many writers to celebrate small-town and rural values: William Humphrey spins wonderful yarns of rural Texas (*The Ordways*), Helen Santmyer looks at a close-knit community in Waynesboro, Ohio ("*. . . And Ladies of the Club*"), and John Gardner sets his characters in *The Sunlight Dialogues* in his own home town of Batavia, New York.

Another one-fourth of the authors were born outside of the United States, primarily in England or other countries of the British Commonwealth. England, second only to New York City, claims 31 authors of *Ameri-*

TABLE 2
Birthplace

Birthplace	Number of Authors
AUTHORS' BIRTHPLACES[a]	
COUNTRIES	
U.S.	142
England	31
Australia	5
Russia, Canada	4 each
India	3 each
Germany, Japan, China, Scotland, Wales	2 each
Ireland, France, Holland, Belgium, Italy, New Zealand, Transylvania, Turkey	1 each
HIGHEST-RANKED STATES	
New York	51
Illinois	14
Pennsylvania	10
Massachusetts	8
California	6
Texas	5
Ohio	5
New Jersey, Maryland	4 each

[a]Based on the 207 authors and coauthors whose birthplaces were reported.

can best sellers. Writers with more exotic birthplaces are often the children of British or American government personnel. They were born in China or Tokyo but returned to be educated at Cambridge or Yale. Unlike the characters that populate the novels, there are few immigrants among the authors.

Exceptions include Elia Kazan, the son of a Greek rug merchant who came to the United States from Constantinople; Isaac Asimov and Ruth Solomon, who immigrated from Russia; and Anaïs Nin, who immigrated from France. Ian de Hartog fled Holland for England during World War II. Bette Bao Lord was the daughter of a Chinese government official who settled in the United States. She went on to be educated at Tufts and the Fletcher School of Diplomacy. Vladimir Nabokov, son of an aristocratic Russian family, went to school in England and became an American citizen at age 45.

Table 2 shows the authors' birthplaces according to country and the highest-ranked American states.[6]

Education and Experience

Facts on education can add to the emerging profile of the best-selling authors. They are on the average a highly educated group. Almost 80% have

TABLE 3
Education and Experience

EDUCATION[a]

Total number of authors attending any college or university: 154

SCHOOLS ATTENDED BY FOUR OR MORE AUTHORS:

Columbia and Barnard	19
Harvard and Radcliffe	16
Yale	10
Oxford	8
Cambridge	4
Universtiy of London	4
Wellesley	4
Stanford	4
City College of New York	4

UNUSUAL EDUCATIONAL EXPERIENCES:

B. Bradford—educated in private schools
Cheever—expelled from Thayer Academy
Christie—educated at home; attended a finishing school
Francis—left school at the age of 15
L'Amour—self-educated
McClary—educated in private schools
Nin—self-educated

[a]Based on the 197 authors and coauthors for which the information was available.

attended a college or university (and about 85% of the American-born authors), compared to the small proportion—about 35%—of the United States population as a whole. See table 3.

It is possible to remain at home, or run off to sea, and still pursue the writing of novels. When John Cheever published his story "Expelled!" in the *New Yorker*, he could argue that he did not need further schooling. However, writers like Cheever or L'Amour are the exception, not the general rule. More typically, the authors have attended some of the most prestigious schools in England and America. For every author with no higher education, there is another with an advanced degree: the economists Galbraith and Erdman; the lawyers Auchincloss and Agnew; the doctors Michael Crichton and Cook; and the scholars Eco, Asimov, Gardner, Irving, and French, to mention a few.

There are few Horatio Alger stories to be found among these authors.[7] While their *characters* go from rags to riches, poverty is not a prominent part of the authors' own biographies. Again, exceptions exist. Baldwin, Michener, Robbins, James—all came from poor beginnings. Holt had to leave secondary school because of a lack of money. She then decided to write books that would sell as widely as possible, and she has been writing them ever since. However, to judge by the facts on education, most authors did not find poverty a serious obstacle at the start of their careers.

By what routes have the authors come to their present position? Many have worked in writing-related jobs, as would be expected. They have been journalists, professors, screenwriters, or have worked for advertising or publishing firms. A much smaller group have used a celebrity gained elsewhere as the basis for their best-selling fiction. They have been vice-presidents, ambassadors, White House assistants, show business personalities. People buy the fiction to read inside accounts or to see what the personalities have to say. A third group have written about their profession—as sailor, soldier, or policeman—becoming an author in the process. A fourth and final group lists no other major occupation. They have become writers of fiction by writing fiction. T. H. White "retired" from his teaching job at the age of 30 to begin work as a writer. Stephen King published stories in college and kept on writing, and publishing, them. Like Cheever, King had no reason to look further for what might be a rewarding career.

The authors can be grouped as follows according to their previous occupation:[8]

	Number of Authors
Authors Only (no other occupation)	52
Other Writers (journalists, professors, screenwriters, others)	107
Celebrities (in show business, politics)	19
Career Changers (doctors, sailors, police, other)	26

The Celebrities stand apart from the other authors. Typically their first novel is written at the midpoint of their career and becomes an immediate best seller. Elia Kazan, for example, already famous as a film director, published *The Arrangement* at the age of 58. Television star Joan Rivers was 47 when her first novel appeared. The Career Changers, in contrast, are considerably younger. They do not take long to use material from one career as a basis for another. Typical examples include Dorothy Uhnak and Robin Cook. The policewoman was 31 when her first novel was published; the doctor was 32.

These are the exceptions, however. Most of the authors have been writers from the beginning. Many publish early—long before their books appear on the best-seller lists. Those who are Authors Only have no other career or reputation to rely on to build the sales of their books. It is not surprising, then, that these writers show the lowest proportion of first novels published as best sellers (six percent). Ross Macdonald was 29 when his first novel was published, and 54 when his first best seller appeared.

The new authors of the 1980s show the same career patterns. There are a few Celebrities and Career Changers. Performer Bette Midler wrote an instant best seller, while Kit Williams, artist and factory worker, produced *Masquerade*. The large majority, however, have worked in other writing professions. Many were already well known; others would become known by their books. Next in frequency are the Authors Only, those for whom fiction writing is a lifetime career. Stephen Donaldson is unusual in producing a best seller only five years after his first novel was published. William Kotzwinkle waited ten years and Louis L'Amour even longer. The record, however, goes to teacher Helen Santmyer. Sixty years after her first novel was published, she made the best-seller list.

A Group Portrait

The authors' group portrait resembles that of other elites in many ways. The authors are middle-aged, highly educated professionals, many of whom have won distinction in previous careers. They are members of middle-class or upper-class families, primarily in England and the large metropolitan areas of the United States. All but James Baldwin are white. However, this portrait is different from others in one striking regard—there are more women in the picture. Overall, about 30% of the authors are women, a rate holding constant from the 1960s to the present. (The British-born authors include even more women proportionately—almost 50%—than the American-born authors do.) In contrast, the media elite and U.S. senators are more than 90% male. Traditionally, more women than men have had the option to work at home and still pursue the writing of fiction. Then, too, the profession of author, unlike many professions, is not held to be the domain of one sex more than the other.

The group portrait is distinctive in another way, too: it allows for great individual variation. For each point of similarity among the authors, we find many exceptions. Some were poor, some were born in the rural South, some are very old or very young. *Adding together* all these exceptions results in the diversity described in the first chapter. Imagine a conversation between Judith Krantz and Agatha Christie—or Louis L'Amour and Louis Auchincloss. Many of the authors have little in common with each other. While most jobs restrict their applicants by age, sex, education, and experience, there are many routes to becoming a best-selling author. Although the group as a whole shows features in common, much diversity remains.

Unique Jobs and Positions

The following is a list of some unusual positions the authors have held. We have selected only the ones that seemed especially unusual or unique.

Adams, D.	Bodyguard
Agnew	Vice-president of the U.S.
Archer	Member of the House of Commons
Auchincloss	Wall Street lawyer
Bach	Flight instructor

Barth	Member of a jazz band
Buck	Missionary
Clancy	Insurance broker
Cook	Ophthalmologist
Cussler	Guide for shipwreck expeditions
Durrell	Director of public relations for the government of Cyprus
Fleming	Assistant director of Naval Intelligence
Francis	Steeplechase jockey
Galbraith	Ambassador to India; economist
Gann	Airline pilot
Gardner, J. E.	Ordained priest in Church of England
Greeley	Ordained Roman Catholic priest
Griffin	Police officer in the Sudan
Hackett	Commander in Chief of the British Army of the Rhine
Heller	Bombardier, 60 missions, World War II
Hersey	Private secretary to Sinclair Lewis
James	Magistrate in London
L'Amour	Light-heavyweight professional boxer; won 51 of 59 fights
le Carre	British Foreign Service officer
McCullough	Teacher in the Australian Outback
MacLean	Investor in pubs in England
Potok	Ordained rabbi
Robbins	From orphan, to millionaire at age 20, to shipping clerk
Safire	Special assistant to President Nixon
Salinger	Press secretary to Presidents Kennedy and Johnson; ambassador
Steel	Mother of nine children
Tarr	Ordained rabbi
Uhnak	Policewoman
Vinge	Salvage archaeologist
Wambaugh	Policeman

Matters of Fact and Fiction

These background facts can be kept in mind in reading the following chapters. The characters, like their authors, are often middle-aged or older. They face midlife crises, or they return from retirement to go on one more mission or solve one final crime. Subject matter, too, is affected by the nationality of the authors. Spy stories, for example, are largely a British import, while books about sex are almost entirely American. Mysteries are written by British women and American men.

Are there other facts about the authors that help in reading the fiction? Only a few of the books are heavily autobiographical. For example, *The Bell Jar* is the story of Sylvia Plath's own life, her beginning career as a writer and the mental illness that culminated in suicide. In *Fathers*, Herbert Gold is the son who writes of his own father and his relationship with him; and Paul Erdman could be the banker in *The Billion Dollar Sure Thing* who becomes caught up in international money deals and finds himself in prison. Erdman began this first novel from a Swiss jail. Solzhenitsyn, too, tells of his own experiences in a Soviet prison in *The First Circle*; and Leon Uris is the best-selling writer involved in a court trial for slandering an ex–Nazi doctor (*QB VII*). James Baldwin tells of his childhood and search for identity (*Tell Me How Long the Train's Been Gone*). Bette Bao Lord returned to China for a reunion with her family and wrote *Spring Moon*.

Other books, while less obviously autobiographical, give a psychological portrait of the author.[9] The fictional hero of *The Arrangement* must confront the same lies and compromises that author Kazan admits to in his own life. In *An American Dream*, Stephen Rojack suddenly kills his wife and plunges into a strange underworld of violence and romantic adventure. Author Norman Mailer stabbed his wife, too, critically but not fatally. Unlike his character, however, Mailer surrendered to the police and was hospitalized briefly.

Theophilus North reflects the optimism and enthusiasm of its author, Thornton Wilder. The fictional Theophilus gets to do what author Thornton wished to do; in fact, Theophilus was the name of Wilder's twin brother, who died at birth. The author's beliefs are given even fuller statement in *The Eighth Day*, where hope becomes a physical force, driving from one generation to the next. There is an intriguing passage halfway through the novel where the elderly Mrs. Wickersham learns of the identity of the fugitive hero John Ashley. "I'm tired of talking. My voice is tired," she says. "Life is a series of promises that come to nothing" (pp. 196, 197). But soon she is feeling 30 years younger and arranging the details of Ashley's escape. One can imagine the novelist, nearing 70, saying the same thing and returning to the same state of hope.

Much more commonly, authors set their fictional characters in situations that they themselves know well. Benchley writes about sharks, de Hartog ships, and Cussler shipwrecks. While Dick Francis tells about horse racing, pilots Serling and Bach write about flying. Robin Cook's main characters are doctors, while officers Wambaugh and Uhnak use detectives. Father Greeley tells about a priest in Chicago who writes a syndicated column. Ambassador Galbraith writes about the State Department, and presidential assistants Safire and Salinger about intrigue in the White House. Spiro Agnew's main character is a vice-president facing resignation and disgrace.

Susann's *Valley of the Dolls* was criticized among other things for its sensational mix of drugs, sex, and Hollywood glamour. But Susann evidently was writing about people she actually knew and recording dialogue that she heard. *Once Is Not Enough*, which adds sadism and incest to the rest of the brew, is drawn from a true-life story. The famous film star on whom the account is based knew Susann and helped her promote the book.[10]

These are only a few of the many examples. Imagine a plot that brings its main character from an orphaned childhood to great fortune at the age of twenty, and then plunges him back to poverty and once more to fame and wealth. This is not the plot of a novel, however, but the life of Harold Robbins. Sidney Sheldon is another author who has lived through extremes of poverty and wealth. An article on the author by *Publishers Weekly* concludes: "If his characters seem larger than life, if his stories seem too full of miracles and good fortune, if the scenes evoke both extreme poverty and spectacular wealth, then Sidney Sheldon is guilty of the same technique of every author—that of drawing from his own life."[11]

Yet there are at least as many books where the character's experience is far from the author's own. Fleming, le Carre, Behn, and Buckley worked with intelligence agencies. (Buckley says he was "affiliated" with the CIA in Mexico.) But other spy writers—Follett, MacInnes, Ludlum, Morris West—had no such background. Trevanian is the pseudonym of a professor of film at a Texas university, and John Gardner, Fleming's successor in writing James Bond stories, had been an ordained priest and a theatre critic.

The same mix is found for books on American politics. While Safire, Agnew, and Salinger had first-hand experience in Washington, Archer, Caldwell, and Wallace did not. Wallace was invited to follow President Kennedy around for 10 days to do research on *The Man*, but that does not make for an inside account. And while Jones, Wouk, and Vonnegut drew on their own experience for books about war, Moore and Patterson did not. Moore was a civilian who trained with the Green Berets and observed them in Vietnam, and Patterson spent three years in peacetime with the Royal Horse Guards.

Of course, "There is private autobiography, and there is public," as Steven Becker writes.[12] The best-known public facts of an author's life may not be the important ones, in terms of the life or the writing. The best characters and scenes are often drawn not from life but from the writer's own imagination. Agatha Christie tells how Miss Marple came into being:

> [She] was not in any way a picture of my grandmother; she was far more fussy and spinsterish than my grandmother ever was. But one thing she did have in common with her—though a cheerful person, she always expected the worst of everyone and everything, and was, with almost frightening accuracy, usually proved right.[13]

There need not be an original Miss Marple. Once created, she has a life of her own.

Nor, to hold to the standards of fiction, does experience ultimately matter. The story can be judged independently of the experience from which it was drawn. Still, it is interesting to see the best-selling mixture of fact and fiction. Celebrities can write about their own lives or entirely different subjects; others can write about them at second hand. Journalists report stories they have covered, do research on ones they wish they had covered, or make them up out of thin air. Intelligence agents, Scottish ladies, and film critics—all write spy stories. To judge by the sales, it does not seem to matter. These very different authors can convince people to care about what they have to say.

On Writing

ANDREW GREELEY

I am telling the kind of story I want to tell, the way I want to tell it, to people who like such stories, and that seems to me quite enough.

(*Confessions of a Parish Priest*, p. 493)

AGATHA CHRISTIE

It was by now just beginning to dawn on me that perhaps I *might* be a writer by profession. I was not sure of it yet. I still had the idea that writing books was only the natural successor to embroidering sofa cushions.

(*An Autobiography*, p. 401)

P. D. JAMES

I did hope eventually to be regarded as a serious novelist, and I felt that mystery writing would be a wonderful apprenticeship because it's a very disciplined form. Then . . . I realized that you can write a book within this framework that has claims to be regarded as a serious novel. You can deal with some of the great realities of human existence and with the society we live in. I like this framework; I suspect that I even need it.

(Book-of-the-Month Club interview, on the publication of
A Taste for Death)

UMBERTO ECO

I began writing *The Name of the Rose* . . . prodded by a seminal idea: I felt like poisoning a monk. I believe a novel is always born of an idea like this; the rest is flesh that is added along the way.

(Postscript to *The Name of the Rose*, as quoted in *World Authors*,
1975–80, p. 205)

LAWRENCE SANDERS

I don't take myself seriously, so why should anyone else? I'm writing entertainment—I hope intelligent entertainment, but that's all.

(Interview, *Publishers Weekly*, August 2, 1976)

FLETCHER KNEBEL

I do not delude myself today about my talents. . . . I regard myself as a journalistic novelist, not a literary one. . . . I enjoy the writing and the reading of novels, but my life has many other interests—politics, travel, group psychology, sports, goofing about, films, holistic health and self-awareness exercises. Oh yes, and poker.

(World Authors, 1975–80, p. 397)

CHAIM POTOK

Just as Faulkner came from the South, I came from Jewish Orthodox. And writers who write seriously, write about what they know best. This is what I know best.

(World Authors, 1975–80, p. 603)

JOHN D. MACDONALD

I want to be intrigued by what is going to happen next. I want the people that I read about to be in difficulties—emotional, moral, spiritual, whatever—and want to live with them while they find their way out of these difficulties. . . . I want to forget the fact that I am writing a book. I want to be in some other place and scene of the author's devising.

(Edgar Hirshberg, *John D. MacDonald*, Boston, Twayne, 1985, p. 46)

RONA JAFFE

Why do I write? I think it's the only way I can survive. It's the way I deal with my life.

(The Writer as Celebrity, p. 96)

LEON URIS

As a writer you've got a shot at making an impact on the world until your dying day, and even beyond. . . . Wise old writers never die. They don't even fade away. They just snarl forever.

(Writer's Digest, August, 1987, p. 40)

ISAAC ASIMOV

I do all my own typing, all my own proofreading, all my own indexing, all my own research, all my own letter writing, all my own telephone answering. I like it that way. Since I don't have to deal with other people, I can concentrate more properly on my work, and get more done.

(Contemporary Authors, New Revision Series 19:31)

JOHN O'HARA

I am a novelist, and a social historian only incidentally. Nevertheless my novels do partake of . . . social history, and behind my decision to make a novel is the question, can I say what I want to say about my times as well as what I want to say about my people, my characters?

(*An Artist Is His Own Fault*, ed. Matthew Bruccoli, pp. 44, 45)

STEPHEN KING

I'll always write because that's what I do best. There are people who go to psychoanalysts for 20 years to try to understand why they have certain interests and feelings. I just indulge them.

(*Time* magazine, August 30, 1982, p. 87)

WILLIAM STYRON

Unless you can make truth and imagination come together, you're not writing anything which is going to live, which is going to have value. . . . To put it down so that when the reader reads it he says, this is the way it is.

(*Conversations with William Styron*, p. 53)

MARY RENAULT

As a historical novelist I have a powerful horror of exploiting the dead. . . . I have tried to fill in the gaps, but never knowingly falsified. I would rather approach the graves of our forebears upon earth as a guardian and servant, than as a tomb-robber.

(*World Authors, 1950–70*, p. 1202)

E. L. DOCTOROW

[Speaking of *Ragtime*] So my answer to the question—Is this really true? Did Morgan really meet Ford? Did Evelyn Nesbit really meet Emma Goldman?—My answer is, they have now, they have all met now.

(*The Book of the Month*, p. 236)

Full citations to all references are given in the bibliographical note at the end of the book.

NOTES

1. See *Statistical Abstract of the U.S.*, 1987, p. 18. Both the 1970 and 1980 census figures show a relatively even distribution for adults in all age groups until age 60.

2. Authors are counted each time they published a book in the 1980s, with the date of birth subtracted from the date of publication.

3. S. Robert Lichter et al., *The Media Elite* (Bethesda, Md.: Adler & Adler, 1986), pp. 20–22. The media outlets are the *New York Times*, the *Washington Post*, the *Wall Street Journal*, *Time*, *Newsweek*, *U.S. News and World Report*, and the news units at CBS, NBC, ABC, and PBS.

4. Each author or coauthor is counted once, for a total of 216. The exception is the multiple authors writing under the name of Penelope Ashe. These are counted as one author. Deaths are taken from the 1988 Cumulative Index to the *Contemporary Authors* series, volume 122, updated where possible. The average figure used is a median.

5. Lichter et al. (p. 22) report that half of the media elite come from the Northeast, 20% from the large industrial states of the Midwest, and only 3% from the Pacific Coast. The authors are similar, with 55% of American-born writers from the Northeast, 16% from the large Middle-Western states, and 7% from the Pacific Coast. The northeastern states are New York, New Jersey, Pennsylvania, and the six New England states. The large midwestern states are Michigan, Illinois, Ohio, and Indiana.

6. All of the states except Maryland could be called high in population (with more than three million residents) based on the 1920 census figures. The 1920s is the median decade of birth for the authors. The only other states with more than three million residents at the time were Missouri and Michigan. Each had one best-selling author.

7. The same point is made about the media elite. See Lichter et al., pp. 20–22.

8. Based on the 204 authors and coauthors with previous occupations listed. Occupations lasting less than three years are not included. Where more than one occupation is cited, an attempt was made to designate one as the primary occupation, choosing a writing career over a non-writing career. Thus journalists Drew Pearson, William Buckley Jr., and Pierre Salinger are included as Other Writers rather than Celebrities. All three published first novels that were also best sellers.

9. See Elia Kazan, *Elia Kazan: A Life* (New York: Knopf, 1988); Gilbert Harrison, *The Enthusiast: A Life of Thornton Wilder* (New York: Ticknor & Fields, 1983); Peter Manso, *Mailer: His Life and Times* (New York: Simon & Schuster, 1985).

10. See Barbara Seaman, *Lovely Me: The Life of Jacqueline Susann* (New York: Morrow, 1987), esp. pp. 291–95 and 422, 423.

11. *Publishers Weekly*, November 25, 1988, p. 54.

12. *Contemporary Authors Autobiography Series*, ed. Dedria Bryfonski, vol. I (Detroit: Gale Research 1984), p. 33.

13. Agatha Christie, *An Autobiography* (New York: Ballantine, 1977), p. 524.

The Categories

MANY PEOPLE CHOOSE their reading by topic or genre. They watch for the new mysteries or read books about war. Therefore, it is useful to provide these categories, if only to give more information as to what the book is about. The books are classified by the standard fictional *genres*: mystery, horror, saga, science fiction, spy, historical novel, western, short stories, and books for young readers. They are also classified by *topic* if the main action involves one of the subjects found so frequently among the best sellers: namely, war, religion, American politics, glamour, sex, and international intrigue without the spies. (Romance was not used as a category because it was so common that it did not provide any meaningful distinction.) Where additional information is needed, three broader categories are used—suspense, adventure, and drama—paralleling the kind of classification often found in movie listings. Drama is used as the residual category for all books not otherwise classified.

Thus the 19th-century tale *True Grit* is classified as a western and a historical novel, while both *Travels with My Aunt* and *The Money-Changers* are called dramas. All books are given some classification, and some books have more than one.

Any classification scheme raises some questions: witness the dispute about whether the tomato is a vegetable or a fruit. Different classifications can be used and different cutoff points assigned. Some books fit more easily in categories than others do. The attempt is not to impose any hard and fast labels on the books, but to make the categories as useful as possible in supplying information. In all cases, of course, the short description of the book, given in chapter 1, will tell more about why the category was used and how well it fits.

The Categories

The following definitions have been followed in describing books by categories. Since no single agreed-on definitions exist, these have been adapted for contemporary fiction from a number of dictionaries and books of literary terms.[1]

I. Genres

HISTORICAL NOVEL:
A story whose primary action occurs in a time before the recent past. We have defined this as occurring before World War I (1914–1918). Sagas beginning in the 19th century and continuing to the present are not included if more than half of the story takes place following 1914. However, books of legendary history, such as the tales about King Arthur, are included whether based on historical fact or not.

HORROR:
A tale relying for its effect on fear of the unknown, typically involving a supernatural threat or one that cannot be explained in terms of ordinary reality or everyday experience.[2] Some natural events are carried to such a bizarre and fearful extreme that they seem best described as horror stories.

MYSTERY:
A story whose primary action involves an enigma to be solved, usually including the commission of a crime. Books about spies and international intrigue are excluded.

SAGA:
A long narrative that chronicles the lives of more than one generation of characters, usually in the same family. The emphasis is on the chronological sequence, from birth and childhood through marriage and childbirth. Books in a series that trace the lives of successive generations are also called sagas. See, for example, Howard Fast's four books about the Lavette family.

SCIENCE FICTION AND FANTASY:
A story based on a premise beyond conventional reality or recognized scientific achievement. Science-fiction writers themselves argue about how

broad or narrow a definition should be used. By this broad definition, *Slaughterhouse-Five* and *Giles Goat-Boy* can be called science fiction, and so would such an earlier classic as *Gulliver's Travels*.

SPY STORY:
A story involving various kinds of espionage or covert activity between governments or subgovernment groups. The agents can be either amateurs or professionals.

The categories of *Short Stories*, *Westerns*, and *Stories for Young Readers* are self-explanatory.

II. Topical Categories

Stories of *war, religion, American politics, glamour, sex*, or *international intrigue*, excluding spy stories. The categories are used only when the topic provides the primary action of the story: mainly in supplying (1) the occupation of a main character, (2) repeated action, or (3) the principal setting. Note that this is a narrow definition of the categories. Books might have a political theme or impact (*Hurry Sundown*; *The Establishment*) without being called books on politics. Books can use scenes of war or sex, as they commonly do, without being called books about these topics.

III. Broader Categories

SUSPENSE:
A story that invokes uncertainty of outcome as one of its main effects, usually placing major characters in high-risk positions. Many of the so-called Gothic novels of romantic suspense are also included if some danger threatens the main characters. Suspense is used only for books not already classified as other kinds of thrillers (mystery, spy story, horror tale).

ADVENTURE:
A story of exciting exploits, typically of a physical nature and out-of-doors. While the characters may be placed in high-risk positions, the emphasis is on the action more than the suspense.

DRAMA:
Broadly defined as a story which portrays life or character, whether serious or comic, involving conflicts and emotions. While most of the books would be included by this definition, it is used primarily for those not otherwise classified. In a few cases, the term is added when a more specific category would be misleading. Thus Graham Greene's *The Human Factor* is called Spy–Drama. People who would not usually read spy novels might enjoy the book even though the major character happens to be a spy.

Suspense and adventure are used only rarely: most books fit within more specific genres. About 80 books altogether are classified only as dramas.

It is worth looking more closely at these dramas to see that they do not contain other obvious categories. There are scattered books (no more than five each) on such subjects as race and social satire. There are tales of policemen and teachers, a gambler, a godfather, and a heart-attack victim. Dramas include Solzhenitsyn's *The First Circle*, Hailey's *Strong Medicine*, and Bach's *Jonathan Livingston Seagull*. They include unique books by such novelists as John Cheever, John Gardner, and Graham Greene. But dramas also include *Summer of '42*; *Love Story*; and *The Saga of Baby Divine*. The term *drama* seems best to describe this variety without trying for any further subdivision.

Patterns in Best-Selling Fiction

Using these categories helps to uncover the patterns in popular fiction: what books have been on the best-seller lists most frequently and how trends have changed across time. The ranking of the various categories is shown in table 4. The table shows the proportion of all the books that fall into each of the categories: that is, how many books have been mysteries as opposed to westerns or spy stories. It also shows how these proportions have changed across the years.

Leading the genres in frequency are the *historical novels*. Highest in popularity in the 1960s, they have held first place through the years to the present. If anything, the percentages understate the attraction of history, since they exclude the sagas focusing on the more recent past. Most of the sagas, listed separately in the table, begin around the turn of the 20th century and concentrate on the years following World War I.

Second in popularity are the *tales of spies and international intrigue*, together making up 15% of the best sellers. Mysteries follow, about as popular as the spy novels considered alone. Since the 1970s, detectives have been doing as much business as spies. But notice also the dramatic increase in science fiction in the most recent years. While these books have always had their share of devoted enthusiasts, they now seem to be reaching a larger audience. Arthur Clarke, Isaac Asimov, Frank Herbert—all have been writing books for years, but they did not become top sellers. Finally, westerns, tales of horror, and children's stories, so popular at the box office,[3] are the least popular among this book-reading audience.

Table 4 also shows how the topics have changed in popularity across time. While sex remains the most popular subject, books on glamour have increased sharply in the 1980s, and books on politics, war, and religion have declined. What could be called the broader social topics—war, politics, religion—outsold the personal topics—sex and glamour—in the 1960s and early 1970s; by the end of the 1970s the situation was reversed. Sex and

TABLE 4

The Trends across Time

| GENRE AND TOPIC | PERCENTAGE OF ALL BOOKS IN EACH CATEGORY[a] | | | | |
	1960s	Early 1970s[b]	Late 1970s	1980s	Total
Historical Novels	17	19	15	17	17
Spy Stories	9	7	12	11	10
International Intrigue	1	9	5	6	5
Mysteries	4	7	10	12	8
Sagas	4	8	12	10	8
Science Fiction	2	1	3	12	4
Horror Stories	1	4	2	5	3
Short Stories	4	1	4	2	3
Juvenile Books	0	0	0	3	1
Westerns	1	0	0	1	—
Books about					
Sex	11	8	12	15	12
American Politics	8	8	7	4	7
War	9	5	9	5	7
Religion	9	7	3	4	6
Glamour	4	3	6	8	5
TOTAL NUMBER OF BOOKS	138	102	113	115	468

[a]Books are counted more than once if they fall into several categories, but the percentage is based on the total number of books. In other words, 8% of all the books can be classified as mysteries, whether or not they also fall into other categories. Books classified as drama, suspense, or adventure are not included in the table.

[b]Through 1974.

glamour, of course, can be treated as broad social issues; however, most of the best sellers do not treat them this way.

Perhaps the most striking revelation in the table is the increase in standard genre fiction across the years: that is, historical novels, spy stories, mysteries, sagas, westerns, science fiction, and horror. These books together totaled about a third of the best sellers in the 1960s, about one-half in the 1970s, and more than 60% in the 1980s. The miscellaneous "dramas" and books on war, politics, and religion have fallen correspondingly. The dramas of the 1980s remain diverse. They include novels by John Gardner and John Updike, contemporary romances by Danielle Steel, and the short joke book on Baby Divine. There are simply fewer of them, proportionately, than there were in the past decades.

Which trend is affecting the other is more difficult to say. As the social and political issues of the 1960s fell from fashion, books on these topics may have become less popular—with readers or publishers or both. But this does not explain why the number of dramas has also decreased. The late 1970s and 1980s were known for their eclectic borrowing of many different styles and fashions. No one theme or subject or style predominated. Faced with such uncertainty about the fashions of the day, publishers